AS THE DOCTRINE PENDULUM SWINGS

By Marion David Moore

MARION DAVID MOORE

Copyright © 2021 by Marion David Moore

Biblical excerpts taken from King James and/or
1901 American Standard Versions of the Bible.

2nd Edition Revised February 2021

PURPOSE

It is the intent of this quarterly to present sound principles of Bible interpretation and provide examples of scripture where these principles apply. Thus, the purpose of this quarterly is to provide truth seekers with the tools they need to properly interpret and understand the Holy Scriptures.

MARION DAVID MOORE

CONTENTS

1 *FROM* ONE EXTREME
   TO THE OTHER 7

2 *FROM* ATHEISM
   TO A WORLD OF DENOMINATIONS 21

3 *FROM* DEISM
   TO CALVINISM 33

4 *FROM* THE SINNER'S PRAYER
   TO A CHRISTIAN'S LACK OF PRAYER 47

5 *FROM* TOTAL SILENCE
   TO USURPING AUTHORITY 57

6 *FROM* NO MUSIC IN WORSHIP
   TO MUSICAL INSTRUMENTS IN WORSHIP 73

7 *FROM* WORDS ALONE DETERMINE IF IT'S
   WORSHIP
   TO LISTENING TO A HYMN IS WORSHIP 83

8 *FROM* WIDOWS CAN MARRY ANYONE
   TO THEY MUST MARRY CHRISTIANS 93

9 *FROM* HETEROSEXUAL FORNICATION
TO HOMOSEXUAL FORNICATION 105

10 *FROM* INFANT BAPTISM
TO ADULT BAPTISM BY
SPRINKLING OR POURING 115

11 *FROM* OLD TESTAMENT IS BINDING TODAY
TO NEW TESTAMENT EPISTLES ARE JUST
LOVE LETTERS 125

12 *FROM* CHURCH WAS AN AFTERTHOUGHT
TO KINGDOM WILL BE ESTABLISHED WHEN
JESUS RETURNS 137

13 *FROM* THE BEGINNING
TO THE END 147

1

FROM ONE EXTREME *TO* THE OTHER

The Doctrine Pendulum

The doctrine pendulum swings from one extreme to the other with the scriptural truth lying somewhere between the two extremes. On one extreme is liberalism, and on the other is legalism. From the prospective of this book, liberalism is defined as loosing where God has not loosed in heaven, and legalism is defined as binding where God has not bound in heaven.

Koine Greek

The New Testament [NT] was originally written in Koine Greek. Studying the NT in its original language is often helpful in correcting misunderstandings of the English translation. In other words, scriptures as expressed in Koine Greek are often more precise and therefore clearer than their English translation. Matthew 16:18-19 is one of many such cases.

Keys of the Kingdom

Jesus said: "[18]And I say also unto thee, That thou art Peter, and upon this rock I will build my church; and the gates of hell shall not prevail against it. [19] And I will give unto thee the keys of the kingdom of heaven: and whatsoever thou shalt bind on earth shall be bound in heaven: and whatsoever thou shalt loose on earth shall be loosed in heaven" [Matthew 16:18-19 KJV]. The same promise of ability to bind and loose [keys of the kingdom] was made to the other apostles in Matthew 18:18.

A misunderstanding in the mind of some individuals is that regardless of what the apostles decided to bind or loose on earth, the God of heaven would approve. However, the Greek tense of the verbs that are translated "shall be bound" and "shall be loosed" indicates that Jesus' apostles would bind and loose whatever had already been bound and loosed in heaven instead of the other way around. Therefore, the apostles' writings should be considered authoritative and worthy of trust and respect.

Scriptural Authority

The "keys of the kingdom" promise was fulfilled when the apostles received the Holy Spirit in Acts 2:1-4 and revealed the doctrine of Christ to mankind by inspiration of the Holy Spirit [2nd Timothy 3:16]. No doubt some respect the authority of the scriptures, but simply misunderstand their meaning. However, a lack of respect for the authority of the Scriptures has resulted in a denominational world [and even some in the Lord's church] that fails to abide in the doctrine of Christ.

The importance of abiding in the doctrine of Christ can readily be seen in 2nd John 1:9 which states: "Whosoever transgresseth, and abideth not in the doctrine of Christ, hath not God. He that abideth in the doctrine of Christ, he hath both the Father and the Son" [KJV].

Failure to abide in the doctrine of Christ can be avoided by not thinking beyond what is written in the scriptures [1st Corinthians 4:6]. In order to not think beyond what is written, Bible students must be able to recognize the difference between doctrine and their opinion about doctrine. Although expressing an opinion is not wrong in itself, one should never attempt to bind an opinion on other Christians. Only NT doctrine can rightly be bound upon Christians.

Hermeneutic Principles

In addition to a proper respect for the authority of the scriptures, the use of sound principles of biblical hermeneutics [science of interpretation] is essential to avoiding the transgression of not abiding in the doctrine of Christ. The Bible student who desires to abide in the doctrine of Christ would do well in recognizing that the Bible authorizes by commands [generic and specific], approved apostolic examples, and necessary inferences.

Biblical Commands

If you treat a generic command as if it is a specific command [or vice versa], you are not abiding in the apostles' doctrine. For example, if you say the generic command to "go" in Matthew 28:19 requires one to go on foot [specific command] because you think the apostles went on foot, you would be thinking beyond what is written [1st Corinthians 4:6]. Christians are commanded to go but they are not told how to go. Therefore, the choice of how to go is left up to the individual.

Another aspect of biblical commands: Some are binding on Christians today while others are not. Common sense is a necessary ingredient in the process of determining which commands apply to all readers and which ones only apply to the people to whom they were originally given. Consider Titus 3:13-14, which states: "13Bring Zenas the lawyer and Apollos on their journey diligently, that nothing be wanting unto them. 14And let ours also learn to maintain good works for necessary uses, that they be not unfruitful" [KJV]. Common sense tells you that Paul's command for Titus to bring Zenas and Apollos was for Titus only and not for all evangelists. However, his instruction to let ours learn to continue good works so they would not be unfruitful is a principle that would apply to all Christians and is supported by other scriptures as well.

Approved Apostolic Examples

In Acts 20:7 there is an approved apostolic example indicating when the Lord's Supper took place: "And upon the first *day* of the week, when the disciples came together to break bread, Paul preached unto them, ready to depart on the morrow; and continued his speech until midnight" [KJV]. The disciples came together on the first day of the week to partake of the Lord's Supper [to break bread]. This occurrence was not merely incidental, but was practiced by the church with the approval of an apostle whose teachings were authorized by the Holy Spirit. Therefore, verse seven is an approved apostolic example, which authorizes partaking of the Lord's Supper on the first day of the week. If you presumptuously partake on any other day, you are thinking beyond what is written [1st Corinthians 4:6], because no other day is authorized for this purpose anywhere in the New Testament scriptures.

Necessary Inferences

A necessary inference is an implicit [not stated] teaching required by explicit [clearly expressed] statements. The Bible explicitly states that Abram and Lot's journey began in the Ur of the Chaldees [Genesis 11:31], which is outside of Egypt, and that they later came up out of Egypt [Genesis 13:1]. Thus the Bible by necessary inference implicitly teaches that Abram and Lot went down into Egypt.

If you conclude that Abram and Lot did not go down into Egypt because the Bible doesn't explicitly say they did, you would be guilty of misinterpreting biblical teaching.

Scriptural Context

Strong's Numbers are usually very helpful in determining the possible meanings of a word in the original languages of the Bible, which are Hebrew for the Old Testament [OT] and Koine Greek for the NT. However, an individual word in the original language can have several meanings and be translated into different English words. For this reason, it is necessary to consider the immediate context in which the word is used in order to determine the proper translation. Furthermore, remote context pertaining to the textual topic under consideration should not be ignored if the Bible student desires a complete understanding. Remote context may be located in a different chapter of the same book, or in an entirely different book of the Bible. For example, Acts 2:38 indicates that one must be baptized in order to receive forgiveness of sin. However, the Bible student would not know that baptism is a burial [the act of plunging, covering, or immersing] except for the remote context of Romans 6:4, which indicates that Christians were buried with Christ in baptism.

Other Helpful Aids

In addition to the use of hermeneutic principles, the heart of the Bible student plays an extremely important role in the interpretation process. A good and honest heart will aid the exegete [one who draws out] in the process of drawing out [exegesis] what the Holy Spirit has breathed into the scripture instead of attempting to prove a preconceived idea or strongly held belief by forcing misguided thoughts into the meaning of the scripture.

Commentaries written by uninspired writers can be helpful, but in most cases the Bible provides its own best commentary. Scriptures that are difficult to understand must be interpreted in harmony with all passages on the same topic, especially the ones that are easier to understand.

Christians on Guard

In order to be successful in "rightly dividing the word of truth" [2nd Timothy 2:15 KJV], Christians must be on guard against deception by the one who "himself is transformed into an angel of light" [2nd Corinthians 11:14 KJV]. Although Satan is not an angel of light, he sometimes makes himself appear to be one.

Satan's effectiveness often depends upon the influence of those who do not utilize sound principles of biblical hermeneutics. Many who participate in the practice of using unsound hermeneutic principles may not even be aware of their involvement, which points out the importance of being knowledgeable pertaining to hermeneutics.

In Dungan's book "HERMENEUTICS" the heading for Sec. 3 on page 5 reads: "A CORRECT HERMENEUTICS WOULD GO FAR TOWARD

HEALING THE DIVISIONS OF THE CHURCH." Incorrect hermeneutics has undoubtedly caused much division in the religious world and the Lord's church as well.

In Conclusion

The primary purpose of "AS THE DOCTRINE PENDULUM SWINGS" is to teach sound principles of hermeneutics and make application of these principles to the interpretation of scripture. To not deal with Satan's deception accomplished through unsound hermeneutics would be synonymous with condoning it or at the very least allowing the deception to continue its destructive influence.

Every Bible student should always remember Paul's remarks to the Corinthians when he said: "And these things, brethren, I have in a figure transferred to myself and *to* Apollos for your sakes; that ye might learn in us not to think *of men* above that which is written, that no one of you be puffed up for one against another" [1st Corinthians 4:6 KJV]. Notice that "*of men*" in the above text is italicized, which means it was not in the Greek manuscript from which the KJV of the New Testament was translated. Based upon the Greek manuscript Paul is admonishing his readers to not think above or beyond that which is written in scripture.

The LORD stated in Isaiah 1:18, "Come now, and let us reason together" [KJV]. Today God reasons with us through His written word. It is the hope of this writer that Bible students can reason together without thinking too highly of their opinions in order to maintain a proper respect for the authority of the scriptures.

Review

1.   From the prospective of this book, what is the definition of liberalism? _________________

____

____

2.   From the prospective of this book, what is the definition of legalism? _________________

____

____

3.   What was the original language of the New Testament? _______________________________

4. Since it is possible to learn what God requires of the Christian by studying the New Testament in the English language, why is it sometimes helpful to study the New Testament in its original language? ___________

____

____

____

5. What does the Greek tense of the verbs "shall be bound" and "shall be loosed" in Matthew 16:18 tell the Bible student about what the apostles would bind and loose on earth? _____

____

____

____

6. Bible authorization is accomplished by what three types of teaching or instruction? ________

____

____

7.   What two kinds of context should the Bible student consider in order to gain a complete understanding of scripture? ________________

____

8.   What type of heart will aid the Bible student in properly understanding the scriptures? ___

____

9.   In 1st Corinthians 4:6, what does Paul admonish his readers not to think beyond?

____

10. In Isaiah 1:18 God said: "Come now, and let us reason together." Through what does God reason with us today? ___________________

____

2

FROM ATHEISM *TO* A WORLD OF DENOMINATIONS

The Doctrine Pendulum

The doctrine pendulum swings from one extreme to the other with the scriptural truth lying somewhere between the two extremes. On one extreme the atheist claims there is no God, and by implication no church that belongs to God. On the other extreme the denominational world claims that all the churches in existence today belong to God.

Atheism

American Atheists, Inc. was founded in 1963 by Madalyn Murray O'Hair. According to the American Atheists' website: *"Atheism* may be defined as the mental attitude which unreservedly accepts the supremacy of reason and aims at establishing a life-style and ethical outlook verifiable by experience and scientific method, independent of all arbitrary assumptions of authority and creeds." In essence, what the above quotation means is that nothing is acceptable to the atheist beyond what can be experienced or proven scientifically, and that man's reasoning is supreme. In other words, there is no God.

Why do atheists claim there is no deity? It may be that the lifestyles of atheists do not conform to the will of God, so they attempt to sooth their conscience by denying God's existence. It is also possible that a devastating event in their life caused them to claim there is no God, because a loving God would not have allowed such an event. Furthermore, the "Theory of Evolution" and "Secular Humanism" may have had an adverse effect on the mind of many atheists.

Denominational World

In view of the fact that Jesus promised to build only one church, why does the denominational world claim that all churches in existence today belong to God? Some have suggested that the one church mentioned in Matthew 16:18 is a universal church consisting of all the denominations. However, the scriptures do not support this explanation. No denominations existed when Jesus established His church. Therefore, they could not have been a part of His church.

Man's View of the Church

Contrary to the apostle Paul's pleading for everyone to speak the same thing and for there to be no divisions, men have established numerous denominations [divisions] that teach many different doctrines. With respect to denominations, men claim that one church is just as good as another. In spite of the fact that the apostles' doctrine teaches only one plan of redemption, the various man-made churches teach a variety of ways to obtain salvation. As a result, many people believe that all who claim to be Christians are going to heaven; they're just going different ways. Every student of the Bible is encouraged to determine God's point of view relative to the church instead of depending upon man's view.

God's View of the Church

Jesus promised to build only one church: "And I say also unto thee, that thou art Peter, and upon this rock I will build my church; and the gates of hell shall not prevail against it" [Matthew 16:18 KJV]. At the risk of pointing out the obvious, notice that the word church is singular.

In opposition to the different doctrines that man-made churches teach, 1st Corinthians 1:10 indicates that the Lord's church should teach only one doctrine: "Now I beseech you, brethren, by the name of our Lord Jesus Christ, that ye all speak the same thing, and *that* there be no divisions among you; but *that* ye be perfectly joined together in the same mind and in the same judgment" [KJV].

With respect to the one church that Jesus promised to build, the Lord added those who should be saved to the church: "Praising God, and having favour with all the people. And the Lord added to the church daily such as should be saved" [Acts 2:47 KJV].

There was only one church in existence at the time Acts chapter two was written, because denominations did not exist. Therefore, Jesus did not add the saved to a denomination. He added the saved to the one church He promised to build, which is the church He purchased with His own blood: "Take heed therefore unto yourselves, and to all the flock, over the which the Holy Ghost hath made you overseers, to feed the church of God, which he hath purchased with his own blood" [Acts 20:28 KJV]. Because He purchased the church with His own blood, it belongs to Him. Therefore, it is appropriate to use the possessive phrase "the church of Christ" to refer to the one church He promised to build because it belongs to Him.

Romans 16:16 states: "Salute one another with an holy kiss. The churches of Christ salute you" [KJV]. The above verse does not have reference to denominations because they did not exist at the time. It is simply a reference to local congregations of the one church that belongs to Christ. Likewise, 1st Corinthians 16:19 [KJV] refers to various congregations throughout Asia that make up the one church that belongs to Christ, and one in particular that met in Aquila and Priscilla's house:

"The churches of Asia salute you. Aquila and Priscilla salute you much in the Lord, with the church that is in their house."

Even though Jesus organized His church according to the pattern found in the New Testament, people have shown their arrogance by deviating from God's plan in almost every aspect. Denominations have changed the name, organization, doctrine, and worship of the church.

Organization of the Church

The Lord's church has no earthly head. In his epistle to the Ephesians, Paul states: "20 Which he wrought in Christ, when he raised him from the dead, and set *him* at his own right hand in the heavenly *places*, 21Far above all principality, and power, and might, and dominion, and every name that is named, not only in this world, but also in that which is to come: 22And hath put all *things* under his feet, and gave him *to be* the head over all *things* to the church, 23Which is his body, the fulness of him that filleth all in all" [Ephesians 1:20-23 KJV]. Jesus reigns from heaven as head of his one body, the church. We know from nature itself that any configuration other than one body with one head is an abnormality. The many churches in the denominational world, which claim to be under the headship of Christ, are an abnormality and a deviation from the New Testament pattern for the church.

God intended for each congregation of the Lord's people to be under the oversight of a plurality of elders. Writing to the elders of the church in Ephesus, Paul stated: "Take heed therefore unto yourselves, and to all the flock, over the which the Holy Ghost hath made you overseers, to feed the church of God, which he hath purchased with his own blood" [Acts 20:28 KJV]. Chapter one of Titus and chapter three of 1st Timothy indicate that the elders who are appointed must meet the qualifications listed therein. Likewise, the deacons who serve under the oversight of their elders are to meet the qualifications listed in chapter three of 1st Timothy.

Furthermore, evangelists and teachers [Ephesians 4:11] assist the elders [pastors] in feeding the church of God that Jesus purchased with His own blood [Acts 20:28]. The apostles and prophets mentioned in Ephesians 4:11 do not exist today because they were part of the apostolic age [infancy of the church] when miraculous gifts were necessary for confirming the revelation of God's word prior to completion of the New Testament [1st Corinthians 13:8-10].

Doctrine of the Church

Numerous denominational doctrines are the source of confusion in the religious world today. All of the various creed books have similarities but are quite different from New Testament doctrine. The various man-made creeds add to or take away from God's word. Adding to or taking away from God's word is forbidden in both the Old and New Testament [Deuteronomy 4:2 and Revelation 22:18-19]. Although the New Testament should be the only source for church doctrine, denominational leaders continue adding to and taking away from the doctrine taught by Jesus' apostles. By not searching the scriptures daily to see if what they are being told is true [Acts 17:11], people allow these destructive heresies to continue.

Worship of the Church

The worship of the church, which is part of the apostles' doctrine, must be in spirit and in truth

[John 4:24]. In spirit requires that acceptable worship must be from the heart and not just going through a ritual. In truth requires that acceptable worship be according to God's word [John 17:17]. Therefore, true worshippers [John 4:23] during the Christian Age must include the following acts of worship: Preaching [2nd Timothy 4:1-4], Praying [1st Corinthians 14:15], Singing [Colossians 3:16], Giving [1st Corinthians 16:2], and the Lord's Supper [Acts 20:7] in their corporate worship.

In Conclusion

As stated previously, atheists have positioned themselves on one extreme while denominations are on the other, but the truth concerning the Lord's church lies somewhere between the two extremes. Quite often it is difficult to take a stand for truth because of family ties or personal lifestyles that are not in harmony with God's will. Although salvation is a personal matter between an individual and God, obtaining salvation can be hindered by associations with denominations that teach false doctrines pertaining to God's plan of redemption.

Review

1. Since atheism claims there is no God, it promotes the idea that the ____________ of man is supreme.

2. Since no denominations existed when Jesus established His church, they could not have been part of the Lord's ____________ mentioned in Matthew 16:18.

3. Contrary to Paul's pleading for there to be no divisions, men have established numerous ____________________, which by definition are all divisions.

4. Denominations have changed just about every aspect of God's ____________ for the church.

5. Jesus is the one ____________ of the church described in the New Testament.

6. God intended for each congregation of the Lord's people to be under the oversight of a ____________ of elders.

7. Before elders and deacons are appointed to serve a local congregation, they must meet the ___________________ given in the New Testament.

8. Adding to or taking away from God's word is ________________ in both the Old and the New Testaments.

9. Worship by members of the Lord's church must be in spirit and in ___________.

10. Worship that is acceptable to God must be in harmony with His _________.

3

FROM DEISM *TO* CALVINISM

The Doctrine Pendulum

The doctrine pendulum swings from one extreme to the other with the scriptural truth lying somewhere between the two extremes. On one extreme is the deist who believes in a God that is indifferent to humanity. On the other extreme is the Calvinist who believes in a God that predestines people to be saved or lost before they are born.

Deism

According to Dictionary.com deism is "belief in a God who created the world but has since remained indifferent to it." Catherine Beyer, states: "Deism is not a specific religion but rather a particular perspective on the nature of God. Deists believe that a creator god does exist, but that after the motions of the universe were set in place he retreated, having no further interaction with the created universe or the beings within it." In other words, God has no involvement with humanity.

There is historical documentation indicating that some of our nation's founders may have been deists. However, whether or not they were deists is not a major concern of this quarterly; the main point is that deism is one of the extremes of so-called "Christianity."

Calvinism

The Theologians & Theology website states: "According to John Calvin, predestination is God's unchangeable decree from before the creation of the world that he would freely save some people [the elect], foreordaining them to eternal life, while the others [the reprobates] would be 'barred from access to' salvation and sentenced to 'eternal death [180, 184]'."

In "A Treatise of the Eternal Predestination of God" John Calvin stated: "I reply that three things are here to be considered: 1) That the eternal predestination of God, by which He decreed, before the Fall of Adam, what should take place in the whole human race and in every individual thereof, was unalterably fixed and determined. 2) That Adam himself, on account of his departure from God, was deservedly appointed to eternal death. 3) And lastly, that in the person of Adam, thus fallen and lost, his whole future offspring were also eternally condemned; but so eternally condemned that God deems worthy the honour of His adoption all those whom He freely chose out of that future offspring" [Grace Online Library]. In other words, Calvinism teaches that some people are predestined to be lost while others are predestined to be saved, and they can't do anything about it one way or the other.

In the same treatise Calvin stated: "Now, if we are not really ashamed of the Gospel, we must of necessity acknowledge what is therein openly declared: that God by His eternal goodwill (for which there was no other cause than His own purpose), appointed those whom He pleased unto salvation, rejecting all the rest; and that those whom He blessed with this free adoption to be His sons He illumines by His Holy Spirit, that they may receive the life which is offered to them in Christ; while others, continuing of their own will in unbelief, are left destitute of the light of faith, in total darkness." In this quote Calvin mentions a special illumination by the Holy Spirit for those God has predestined to be saved [the elect]. According to Calvinism this illumination generates faith in the elect prior to hearing the gospel and is superior to the preaching of the gospel.

The previous quotes by Calvin pertaining to predestination have been included in this quarterly because there are those who defend Calvin by suggesting that he didn't really believe the doctrines attributed to him by his critics.

Truth about Predestination

Contrary to the deist's belief, God is involved in the lives of human beings. In one sense God does predestine who will be saved and lost, but not in the way Calvinism alleges. Ephesians 1:3-5 states:

"[3]Blessed *be* the God and Father of our Lord Jesus Christ, who hath blessed us with all spiritual blessings in heavenly *places* in Christ: [4]According as he hath chosen us in him before the foundation of the world, that we should be holy and without blame before him in love: [5] Having predestinated us unto the adoption of children by Jesus Christ to himself, according to the good pleasure of his will," [KJV]. According to verse 5, God has predestined us, but when and how? Verse 4 indicates the choosing or predestination occurred before the foundation or creation of the world. In other words, God had a plan for redeeming lost humanity that He established before the beginning of time. However, the how of predestination hasn't been addressed yet.

Romans 8:30 states: "Moreover whom he did predestinate, them he also called: and whom he called, them he also justified: and whom he justified, them he also glorified" [KJV]. Verse 30 provides the steps that are taken in the process of predestination.

God calls by the gospel as 2nd Thessalonians 2:14 indicates: "Whereunto he called you by our gospel, to the obtaining of the glory of our Lord

Jesus Christ" [KJV].

Having been called by the gospel, we are "justified freely by his grace through the redemption that is in Christ Jesus" [Romans 3:24 KJV]. The redemption that is in Christ Jesus required the shedding of Jesus' blood: "Much more then, being now justified by his blood, we shall be saved from wrath through him" [Romans 5:9 KJV].

The shedding of Jesus' blood enables the lost to be "justified by faith" [Romans 5:1 KJV]. In order to be a saving faith, it must be an obedient faith: "By whom we have received grace and apostleship, for obedience to the faith among all nations" [Romans 1:5 KJV]. In other words, one's personal faith must be in harmony with the system of faith [gospel] mentioned in Ephesians 4:4 in order for one to be justified by faith.

In the Christian Age God doesn't arbitrarily choose to save some and condemn others, but rather chooses to save those who are obedient to the gospel. Those who aren't willing to obey are condemned by their own disobedience. If He arbitrarily chose to save some while rejecting others, that would make Him a respecter of persons, which He isn't: "[34] Then Peter opened *his* mouth, and said, of a truth I perceive that God is no respecter of persons: [35] But in every nation he that feareth him, and worketh righteousness, is accepted with him" [Acts 10:34 KJV]. Working righteousness is synonymous with obedience to the gospel as Romans 1:16-17 indicates: "[16] For I am not ashamed of the gospel of Christ: for it is the power of God unto salvation to every one that believeth; to the Jew first, and also to the Greek. [17] For therein is the righteousness of God revealed from faith to faith: as it is written, The just shall live by faith" [KJV].

A Choice in the Matter

As seen in the previous scriptures, God doesn't predestine some to be saved and others to be lost without giving the individuals a choice in the matter. Similar to the forced predestination previously discussed is the belief that God forces individuals to take action in order to accomplish his purpose. Some students of the Bible believe that God is the cause when in reality He has permitted the situation to occur rather than force the occurrence. This brings up the need to define the hermeneutic term metonymy.

Metonymy

Metonymy is where one terminology is substituted in place of another. For example, on page 285 of his book titled *"HERMENEUTICS"* Dungan states: "Many times actions are said to be performed when they have only been permitted, or even foretold". An example of metonymy is found in 2nd Thessalonians 2:11-12 which states: "11And for this cause God shall send them strong delusion, that they should believe a lie: 12 That they all might be damned who believed not the truth, but had pleasure in unrighteousness" [KJV]. The hearts of these individuals had pleasure in unrighteousness and believed not the truth. God, who knows the hearts of men, knew they were receptive to strong delusion and allowed them to believe a lie. Thus the metonymy: the terminology "God shall send them strong delusion" was substituted in place of "God allowed them to receive a strong delusion."

God was not the cause of the strong delusion, but he permitted them to believe a lie. The condition of their heart was the real cause. Anyone who has pleasure in unrighteousness and believes not the truth will be receptive to strong delusion. This interpretation is supported by James 1:13

which states: "Let no man say when he is tempted, I am tempted of God: for God cannot be tempted with evil, neither tempteth he any man" [KJV]. God would never cause anyone to believe a lie by actually sending them a strong delusion, because only truth proceeds from God, as John 17:17 indicates: "Sanctify them through thy truth: thy word is truth" [KJV]. Furthermore, it is impossible for God to lie as Hebrews 6:18 indicates: "That by two immutable things, in which *it was* impossible for God to lie, we might have a strong consolation, who have fled for refuge to lay hold upon the hope set before us" [KJV].

Another example of metonymy is found in 1st Samuel 10:9 which states: "And it was *so*, that when he had turned his back to go from Samuel, God gave him another heart: and all those signs came to pass that day" [KJV]. The condition of Saul's heart changed, but a new heart was not forced upon Saul by God. Saul's heart was changed by the effect of Samuel's word and the fulfillment of the signs. Thus the metonymy: The terminology "God gave him another heart" was substituted in place of "God permitted his heart to be changed by the effect of Samuel's words and the fulfillment of the signs."

A third example of metonymy that involves the hardening of Pharaoh's heart is found in Exodus chapters seven and eight. In Exodus 7:3 [KJV] God says: "And I will harden Pharaoh's heart, and multiply my signs and my wonders in the land of Egypt." In Exodus 8:15 [KJV] the Bible states: "But when Pharaoh saw that there was respite, he hardened his heart, and hearkened not unto them; as the LORD had said." Verse 15 indicates that after he saw the frogs were gone, Pharaoh hardened his own heart and refused to let the Israelites leave.

First, God said He would harden Pharaoh's heart, and then the Bible says that Pharaoh hardened his own heart. So, which was it? Do we have a contradiction or is this simply a metonymy? Obviously Pharaoh's heart was hardened, but how was it accomplished? In reality, God permitted Pharaoh's heart to be hardened each time Egypt experienced a temporary respite [relief] from the plagues. Thus the metonymy: The terminology "God hardened Pharaoh's heart" was used instead of stating that God permitted Pharaoh's heart to be hardened by the "respite."

In Conclusion

In view of the scriptures studied in this chapter, the reader should be able to discern that God does not predestine some to be saved and others to be lost without them being able to do anything about it one way or the other. However, God did predestine before creation that those who obey the gospel would be saved while those who fail to obey would be lost.

Likewise, God does not force individuals to obey in order to accomplish His purpose. In the case of the metonymies previously discussed, God foretold and permitted the situations to occur. He accomplished His will in the process of allowing these situations to occur. God can use both good and evil that exist in the world to providentially accomplish His eternal purpose without forcing His will on those involved.

Review

1. Deism teaches that once God created the universe and its inhabitants, He no longer had anything to do with His creation. True/False

2. According to John Calvin's teaching, people are predestined to be saved or lost, and there is nothing they can do about it one way or the other. True/False

3. Before the beginning of time God did not have a plan of redemption for mankind. True/False

4. In order to be a saving faith, the faith of an individual must be in harmony with the system of faith mentioned in Ephesians 4:4, which is the gospel. True/False

5. The working righteousness mentioned in Acts 10:34 is not synonymous with obedience to the gospel. True/False

6. Metonymy is a figure of speech where one terminology is substituted in place of another. True/False

7. An example of metonymy is where an action is said to have been performed when it has actually been allowed to happen. True/False

8. God was not the cause of the strong delusion mentioned in 2nd Thessalonians 2:11-12; the condition of their heart was the actual cause. True/False

9. In 1st Samuel 10:9, the condition of Saul's heart did change, but it was Samuel's words and fulfillment of the signs that actually caused the change. True/False

10. God forces individuals to obey in order to accomplish His purpose. True/False

4

FROM THE SINNER'S PRAYER *TO* A CHRISTIAN'S LACK OF PRAYER

The Doctrine Pendulum

The doctrine pendulum swings from one extreme to the other with the scriptural truth lying somewhere between the two extremes. On one extreme is the mistake alien sinners [non-Christians] make by believing they can receive forgiveness of sin by praying the "Sinner's Prayer". On the other extreme is the mistake some Christians make by not realizing the need to pray to the Father in heaven for the forgiveness of sin.

Sinner's Prayer

Although there are variations of the sinner's prayer, it basically teaches that alien sinners can be saved by praying for Jesus to come into their hearts and save them without any further action on the alien sinner's part. After painting the "Sinner's Prayer" on the side of a pickup truck, the driver was asked where the sinner's prayer could be found in the scriptures. He admitted that it was not in the Bible.

Many people in the denominational world believe that the sinner's prayer is taught somewhere within the pages of God's word. What scriptural authority is there for teaching that the alien sinner can be saved by praying the sinner's prayer? There is none. Neither the sinner's prayer nor its concept is found within the pages of the New Testament.

Not by the Sinner's Prayer

The mistake made by alien sinners who pray the "Sinner's Prayer" to receive forgiveness of sin can easily be observed from a study of New Testament scripture. There was a devout Gentile named Cornelius who always prayed to God. Acts 10:1-2 [KJV] states: "1 There was a certain man in Caesarea called Cornelius, a centurion of the band called the Italian *band*, 2 *A* devout *man*, and one that feared God with all his house, which gave much alms to the people, and prayed to God alway." Yet his prayers were not sufficient to provide him with forgiveness of sin. Cornelius was told in a vision to send for Simon Peter who would tell him what he ought to do.

When Simon Peter arrived at Cornelius' house, Cornelius said to him: "33 Immediately therefore I sent to thee; and thou hast well done that thou art come. Now therefore are we all here present before God, to hear all things that are commanded thee of God." [Acts 10:33 KJV]. After Peter preached Jesus unto Cornelius' household, he "commanded them to be baptized in the name of the Lord." [Acts 10:48 KJV]. Later when Peter was describing to the Christians in Jerusalem what had happened to Cornelius, he said: "13 And he shewed us how he had seen an angel in his house, which stood and said unto him, Send men to Joppa, and call for Simon, whose surname is Peter; 14 Who shall tell thee words, whereby thou and all thy house shall be saved." [Acts 11:13-14 KJV]. So from these verses it may be observed that when Peter told them words whereby "they shall be saved," they were told "to be baptized in the name of the Lord." Cornelius and his household believed Peter's teaching, so they obtained salvation by obeying what they were taught.

What Peter told Cornelius and his household was consistent with what he told the Jews in Acts 2:38, which states: "[38] Then Peter said unto them, Repent, and be baptized every one of you in the name of Jesus Christ for the remission of sins," [KJV]. The Jews believed Peter, so they obtained remission of sins by repenting and being baptized.

Obviously Cornelius was a penitent believer, because he was told to be baptized in order to be saved. Neither the Jews nor Cornelius' household gained forgiveness of sin by praying the "Sinner's Prayer." Both groups were alien sinners who were saved by obeying the gospel of Christ preached by Peter, which included belief, repentance, and baptism.

Observe All Things

In Matthew 28:20 Jesus instructed his apostles

to teach all nations, baptize them, and teach them to observe all things I have commanded you. That which Jesus commanded his apostles included His instructions pertaining to prayer. Not only did Jesus teach His apostles to pray to the Father [Luke 11:2], but He also set the example for them in His prayer to the Father [John 17].

Likewise, Paul writing to the Colossians instructed them: "And whatsoever ye do in word or deed, *do* all in the name of the Lord Jesus, giving thanks to God and the Father by him" [Colossians 3:17 KJV]. To do something in the name of the Lord Jesus is to do it by His authority or as He has authorized in scripture.

In keeping with his own instructions, Paul stated: "I thank my God through Jesus Christ" [Romans 1:8 KJV]. He also stated: "Likewise the Spirit also helpeth our infirmities: for we know not what we should pray for as we ought: but the Spirit itself maketh intercession for us with groanings which cannot be uttered" [Romans 8:26 KJV].

Different Roles

Based upon the previous scriptures, we ought to pray to the Father, through Jesus [by His authority], with the Spirit making intercession for us. In other words, these scriptures specify the role each person of the Godhead plays in the Christian's prayer life. Therefore, Christians should pray in a manner that is consistent with the role of each member of the Godhead as specified in scripture.

Not Realizing the Need

The mistake made by Christians who don't maintain a prayerful attitude should be obvious from a study of New Testament scripture. Acts 8:22 [KJV] indicates that a Christian should repent and pray for forgiveness: "Repent therefore of this thy wickedness, and pray God, if perhaps the thought of thine heart may be forgiven thee." Repentance and prayer for God's forgiveness go hand in hand.

Likewise, walking in the light and confession of sin to God are both necessary in order for the Christian to be cleansed of all unrighteousness. 1st John 1:7-9 (KJV) states: "7 But if we walk in the light, as he is in the light, we have fellowship one with another, and the blood of Jesus Christ his Son cleanseth us from all sin. 8 If we say that we have no sin, we deceive ourselves, and the truth is not in us. 9 If we confess our sins, he is faithful and just to forgive us *our* sins, and to cleanse us from all unrighteousness." Christians who realize that the blood of Christ continues to cleanse those who are walking in the light need to realize that praying without ceasing [1 Thess. 5:17] is a part of walking in the light. Praying without ceasing doesn't mean that we must spend every waking minute in prayer, but points out the need to maintain a prayerful attitude by praying regularly as the need and opportunity presents itself.

In Conclusion

Both Jews and Gentiles, who were alien sinners, received salvation when they obeyed the gospel of Christ taught by His apostles. There is no example in scripture of an alien sinner obtaining salvation by praying the "Sinner's Prayer". Every example of conversion to Christianity in the New Testament involved obedience to the gospel. Therefore, everyone who wants to obtain forgiveness of sin today will do what the Jews and Gentiles did throughout the book of Acts. Following the error taught in the "Sinner's Prayer" has never and will never save anyone.

Once people become Christians, they have the

privilege and responsibility to maintain a prayerful attitude at all times. Prayer should be addressed to the Father, in the name of Christ [by His authority], with the Holy Spirit making intercession. When Christians pray in this manner, their prayers are consistent with the role for each member of the Godhead that is specified in scripture. Not only did Christ teach His apostles to pray to the Father, but He provided an example by doing the same Himself. In all things Christians should follow Paul's admonition to: "Be ye imitators of me, even as I also am of Christ" [1 Corinthians 11:1 ASV].

Review

1. The sinner's prayer is not found in the
    ___________.

2. Is the sinner's prayer authorized in the scriptures? Yes/No

3. What did Peter tell Cornelius to do in order to be saved? ____________________________
    ________________________________.

4. Cornelius was saved in the same manner the Jews were on Pentecost in Acts 2. True/False

5. Jesus taught his disciples to pray to the ________________.

6. Did Paul state on several occasions that he prayed to the Father?   Yes/No

7. Paul taught that we pray to the Father through Jesus (by Jesus' authority). True/False

8. Some Christians don't realize the need to maintain a ____________________ attitude.

9. Walking in the light is necessary in order for a Christian to continue gaining forgiveness of sin. Yes/No

10. Praying without ceasing means praying regularly as the need and opportunity presents itself.   True/False

5

FROM NO RESTRICTIONS _TO_ ABSOLUTE SILENCE

The Doctrine Pendulum

The doctrine pendulum swings from one extreme to the other with the scriptural truth lying somewhere between the two extremes. On one extreme is the opinion that there are no restrictions on women relative to leadership roles in the Lord's church. On the other extreme is the opinion that women must maintain absolute silence in the worship assembly and are even prohibited from teaching men in private.

The Two Extremes

Many in the denominational world and even some in churches of Christ are promoting the idea that women can assume any role in the church without violating the New Testament scriptures. In an effort to correct this doctrinal error, some have failed to abide in the doctrine of Christ [2nd John 1:9]. As a result, they go beyond what is written in the scriptures [1st Cor. 4:6] and end up at the opposite extreme, claiming that women must maintain absolute silence in the church when men are present.

Restrictions for Women

There should be no doubt that God placed restrictions on women as evidenced by 1st Timothy 2:11-12 which states: "Let the woman learn in silence with all subjection. But I suffer not a woman to teach, nor to usurp authority over the man, but to be in silence" [KJV]. However, the question that must be answered is under what circumstances or to what extent does the Bible restrict women's role?

Meaning Plus Context

In order to determine the meaning of a

biblical text, both the meaning of words in the original language and the context in which they are used should be considered. Although there is nothing wrong with reading commentaries written by uninspired men, the best commentary is found in the biblical context. Some Bible students make the mistake of considering the immediate context while ignoring the remote context. Both the immediate and the remote context should be considered in order to have a full or complete understanding of the scripture.

Worship Assembly

In 1st Corinthians 14:23 when the New Testament writer mentions that: "If therefore the whole church be come together into one place"[KJV], he is speaking of the whole church assembled for a formal worship service and not a situation where members of the church are divided into Bible classes or discussion groups.

Like "the whole church" in verse 23, "the churches" in verse 34 of chapter 14 has reference to congregations or assemblies of the Lord's people as a whole and not to situations where the church is divided into Bible classes or discussion groups.

Neither a biblical discussion group sitting around the dining room table nor a biblical discussion group in a classroom of the church building can accurately be described as "the whole church be come together into one place" [1st Corinthians 14:23]. The fact that a woman is to keep silence in the worship assembly doesn't necessarily require her to keep silent in every situation.

First Adam Then Eve

The inspired writer of 1st Timothy 2:8-14 states: "8I will therefore that men pray every where, lifting up holy hands, without wrath and doubting. 9 In like manner also, that women adorn themselves in modest apparel, with shamefacedness and sobriety; not with broided hair, or gold, or pearls, or costly array; 10 But (which becometh women professing godliness) with good works. 11 Let the woman learn in silence with all subjection. 12 But I suffer not a woman to teach, nor to usurp authority over the man, but to be in silence. 13 For Adam was first formed, then Eve. 14And Adam was not deceived, but the woman being deceived was in the transgression" [KJV].

The fact that Paul indicated the restrictions in

1st Timothy 2:8-14 were based upon the order of creation and the woman being deceived by Satan does not preclude his making a specific application to the worship assembly of the church.

Guidelines for Congregations

In chapter one of 1st Timothy, Paul reminds Timothy why the apostle left him with the church in Ephesus. In chapters two and three Paul gives Timothy guidelines for congregations including qualifications for elders, deacons and their wives.

In 1st Timothy 2:8 Paul says: "I will therefore that men pray every where". The literal translation of the Greek in 1st Timothy 2:8 is as follows: "I will therefore to pray the men in every place." The sentence structure in Greek is different from the normal arrangement of the words in English, but don't let that confuse you. Notice that the definite article "the" is not found in the KJV translation as it is in the literal translation shown above. What Paul is saying is that he wills the men to pray everywhere as opposed to the women praying everywhere. The Greek word that is translated "men" does not mean mankind, but refers to the sex of the persons Paul wants to pray everywhere. The implication is that Paul is speaking about leading prayer in public, because all Christians [men and women] are taught by Jesus to pray privately; e.g., "when thou prayest, enter into the closet" [Matthew 6:6 (KJV)]. The fact that God has given women a submissive role [1st Timothy 2:11] and men a leadership role [Ephesians 5:23], it logically follows that He wants men to lead public prayers.

Modest Apparel

After giving men instructions for public worship, Paul then turns to the women of the congregation expressing the fact that it is appropriate for women professing godliness to adorn themselves with modest apparel [1st Timothy 2:9]. However, neither the reference to men praying everywhere or women adorning modest apparel in 1st Timothy 2 prevents the chapter from being about the church. It is the total context [immediate and remote] of 1st Timothy 2 and 1st Corinthians 14 that aids in determining the proper interpretation of these passages.

Immediate & Remote Context

Consider 1st Timothy 3:14-15 [KJV] which states: "14 These things write I unto thee, hoping to come unto thee shortly: 15 But if I tarry long, that thou mayest know how thou oughtest to behave thyself in the house of God, which is the church of the living God, the pillar and ground of the truth." When Paul says: "These things write I unto thee", he is speaking of the rules for the congregation that he gave Timothy in the previous verses of 1st Timothy. Notice that he wrote those things so it would be known how to behave in the church. Therefore, the context of chapters 1-3 of 1st Timothy is describing how "to behave" in the church.

Now consider 1st Corinthians 14:33-34 (KJV) which states: "33For God is not *the author* of confusion, but of peace, as in all churches of the saints. 34Let your women keep silence in the churches: for it is not permitted unto them to speak; but *they are commanded* to be under obedience, as also saith the law." Notice that the immediate context of 1st Corinthians 14 doesn't specifically state that it is about how "to behave" in the church. Even so, 1st Corinthians 14 is obviously about how to behave in the church [e.g., "Let your women keep silence in the churches: for it is not permitted unto them to speak; but *they are commanded* to be under obedience"]. Although 1st Corinthians 14 and 1st Timothy 1-3 are in different books of the Bible, they serve as remote context for each other because all of these chapters are about how "to behave" in the church. A side-by-side comparison makes it more evident to the discerning eye that the teachings are the same.

Side–By-Side Comparison

1st Corinthians 14	1st Timothy 2
Let your women keep silence in the churches	Let the woman learn in silence
it is a shame for women to speak in the church	with all subjection
it is not permitted unto them to speak	I suffer not a woman to teach
they are commanded to be under obedience	nor to usurp authority over the man

A similar comparison can be found in an article by Alan E. Highers on page 25 of the January 1996 issue of "The Spiritual Sword." He points out that

"There has been a tendency among brethren to apply 1 Timothy 2:11, 12 to present-day problems and to relegate 1 Corinthians 14: 34, 35 to the age of miracles. An analysis of these passages will demonstrate, however, that the same fundamental principles are involved in both passages."

In writing to the various churches, Paul taught the same basic doctrine in all of his epistles even though the wording may not have been exactly the same in every epistle. For example, Paul indicated that the things he wrote to the Corinthians were the commandments of the Lord [1st Corinthians 14:37]. Also, Paul indicated that he left Timothy in Ephesus to charge some in the church that they teach no other doctrine [1st Timothy 1:3].

Absolute Silence or Limited?

In the previous verses the apostle Paul is taking the general principle of women's submissive role as expressed in Genesis 3:16 and making application to the assembly of the church. A woman is not to teach a man or usurp authority over a man in the worship assembly. Instead she is to keep silence or learn in silence. This being the case, it still needs to be determined whether the silence is absolute or limited. At the risk of being overly repetitious, the reader is reminded that the meaning of a text is not determined by the definition of words alone, but by both definition and context.

In 1st Corinthians 14:34 where the women are instructed to "keep silence in the churches", the English term "keep silence" is translated from the Greek word *"σιγαω"*. If women in the assembly of the congregation are to keep absolute silence and not speak at all, then they would not be able to sing songs, hymns, and spiritual songs, confess public sins, or confess the name of Christ prior to baptism. Would anyone forbid women to obey God in the ways just mentioned while in the presence of the congregation?

The same Greek word *"σιγαω"* that is used in 1st Corinthians 14:34 to instruct women to "keep silence" is also used in 1st Corinthians 14:28 to instruct men to "keep silence". If the definition alone [without the context] requires women to not speak at all during the worship assembly, it would also require men to not speak at all during the assembly. However, neither is the case.

1st Corinthians 14:27-28 states: "[27] If any man

speak in an *unknown* tongue, *let it be* by two, or at the most *by* three, and *that* by course; and let one interpret. [28] But if there be no interpreter, let him keep silence in the church; and let him speak to himself, and to God." In verse 28 the men are told to "keep silence", but that doesn't mean they can't speak at all during the worship assembly. Instead they must "keep silence" when the circumstance requires it [e.g., when there is no interpreter]. The reason given is to avoid confusion.

Likewise, women must "keep silence" during the worship assembly when the circumstance requires it [e.g., when she would assume the role of preacher/teacher or otherwise be usurping authority over a man]. The reason given is that she is to be under obedience.

Although 1st Corinthians 14 and 1st Timothy 2-3 are dealing with conduct in the worship assemblies, the general principle found in Genesis 3:16 would suggest that she maintain a submissive role even in a private situation.

Priscilla and Aquila

One private situation that often comes up when discussing women's role in the church is the example of Aquila and Priscilla teaching Apollos. Acts 18:26 (KJV) states: "[26]And he began to speak boldly in the synagogue: whom when Aquila and Priscilla had heard, they took him unto *them*, and expounded unto him the way of God more perfectly." The claim some make is that only Aquila taught Apollos. Notice that the scripture doesn't say that they took him unto them and he taught him. The pronoun "they" in Acts 18:26 is the subject of the verb "took" and the verb "taught", which implies that both Aquila and Priscilla taught Apollos. In the Greek text both the verb that is translated "took" and the verb that is translated "taught" are in the third person plural, which requires the use of the third person plural pronoun "they". Interpretation of this scripture should take into consideration the grammar of the text as well as other remote texts concerning the roles of men and women. With this in mind, "they" [both Aquila and Priscilla] "taught" Apollos privately. When Aquila and Priscilla taught Apollos privately, Priscilla would have done so in a manner that would have maintained her submissive role relative to the men [Gen. 3:16].

Women Prophets

Another teaching situation in the early church involved women prophesying. Since prophesying is in essence teaching, female prophets [1 Corinthians 11:5] would have found it necessary to use their God given ability in such a way as to comply with Paul's instruction for women not to teach or usurp authority over a man in the worship assembly. Even in a private situation, the women who prophesied would have maintained their submissive role. Anyone who would deny women the right to teach men under any circumstances would in essence have denied them the right to teach via prophesy in the first century church. Such a denial would contradict Act 2:17, which specifically states that both sons and daughters would prophesy. In fulfillment of this prophesy, Acts 21:9 indicates that Phillip's daughters did prophesy, but no doubt they prophesied in a way that would have maintained their submissive role.

In Conclusion

The apostles' doctrine does not allow women to usurp authority over a man by serving as a preacher/teacher in the worship assembly. A woman's silence in the worship assembly of the church is limited, not absolute. In order for women to obey God, they can't be required to remain absolutely silent in the worship assembly. They must be able to sing songs, hymns, and spiritual songs, confess their sins, and confess Christ before baptism. Also they must be allowed to teach privately in order to avoid contradicting scripture related to women prophesying, which is a form of teaching. Teaching by miraculous means including prophesying was practiced in order to prove the message was from God during the infant stage of the church's establishment. However, it was no longer practiced following the completion of the New Testament since the source of scripture was firmly established by that time.

Review

1.   Who placed restrictions on women's role in the church? _________________

2.   What two things should be considered in order to determine the meaning of a biblical text? _________________________________

3.   What reasons did Paul give for the restrictions on women found in 1st Timothy 2:8-14? _______

____

____

4.   In 1st Timothy 2:8, does the Greek word that is translated men have reference to mankind (which would include women) or the sex of the persons Paul wants to lead in prayer everywhere? _______________

____

____

5.   What is the definition of immediate context?

____

____

____

6.   What is the definition of remote context?

____

____

____

7.	Under what circumstances are women required to be silent in the worship assembly?

____

____

____

____

8.	In Acts 18:26, what two people taught Apollos? ___________________________

9.	Even when she and Aquila were teaching Apollos privately, what would Priscilla have to maintain? _________________________

____

10.	In essence, prophesying is what? __________

____

6

FROM NO MUSIC IN WORSHIP *TO* MUSICAL INSTRUMENTS IN WORSHIP

The Doctrine Pendulum

The doctrine pendulum swings from one extreme to the other with the scriptural truth lying somewhere between the two extremes. On one extreme is the opinion that churches of Christ do not have music in their worship. On the other extreme is the opinion that mechanical instruments of music used in denominational worship are acceptable to God.

For example, a member of a denomination may ask: "Your church doesn't have music in your worship do you?" Implied in the question is the opinion that singing is not music. Then he may ask: "Do you condemn other churches for using a piano?" Most likely, this question would be prompted by the opinion that mechanical instruments of music in worship are acceptable to God.

Two Kinds of Music

The idea that churches of Christ do not have music in their worship is a misunderstanding of what the term music encompasses. Music can be produced by either mechanical instruments or human voices. In reality, churches of Christ utilize vocal music [i.e., singing] in worship. Many denominations use two kinds of music: vocal music and instrumental music. In view of God's desire for Christians to worship in spirit and in truth [John 4:24], what does God's word teach pertaining to music in worship?

Silence of the Scriptures

A hermeneutic principle, which hasn't been discussed previously, is that silence of the scriptures in conjunction with a specific command is prohibitive relative to other things of equal class. For example, when the Old Testament scriptures indicated that the priests were to be selected from the tribe of Levi and were silent pertaining to the other tribes, God did not have to indicate that priests shall not be selected from the other tribes, because the silence of the scriptures in conjunction with the specific command was prohibitive.

A reference to this principle is found in Hebrews 7:14 [KJV] which states: "For *it is* evident that our Lord sprang out of Judah; of which tribe Moses spake nothing concerning priesthood." Moses' silence relative to Judah prohibited taking the priesthood from Judah because of the specific command to take the priesthood from the tribe of Levi [Numbers 18:6].

Jesus, who was of the tribe of Judah, could not serve as our high priest without a change of the law. When the Law of Moses was done away with and the New Testament [NT] came into effect [Hebrews 9:11, 16], Jesus was no longer prohibited from serving as our high priest.

New Testament Example

The specific command to sing in NT worship is found in Colossians 3:16 which states: "Let the word of Christ dwell in you richly in all wisdom; teaching and admonishing one another in psalms and hymns and spiritual songs, singing with grace in your hearts to the Lord" [KJV]. However, the use of mechanical instruments in worship isn't mentioned anywhere in the NT.

Therefore, the silence of the NT scriptures relative to the use of mechanical instruments in worship in conjunction with the specific command to sing in worship prohibits the use of mechanical instruments in worship.

Common Response

A common response from those who include mechanical instruments of music in their worship is "The scriptures don't say not to play musical instruments in worship." If the NT scriptures had given a general command to make music in worship, both singing and instrumental music in worship would have been acceptable to God. However, the general command to make music in worship isn't mentioned in the NT. Therefore, NT silence relative to the use of mechanical instruments of music in worship in conjunction with the specific command to sing in worship prohibits the use of mechanical instrument of music in worship. As a result, the NT doesn't have to say that mechanical instruments shall not be played in NT worship.

Other References to Music

Like Colossians 3:16, Ephesians 5:19 refers to music in worship: "Speaking to yourselves in psalms and hymns and spiritual songs, and making melody in your heart to the Lord" [KJV]. When members of the church speak to one another in spiritual songs, they are teaching and encouraging each other through their singing. Mechanical instruments of music may entertain people, but they are not acceptable to God, because the only instrument authorized in the New Testament for making melody in worship is the heart.

Hebrews 2:12 takes the idea a step further by: "Saying, I will declare thy name unto my brethren, in the midst of the church will I sing praise unto thee" [KJV]. Notice that the singing of praises to God referenced in verse 12 occurs in the midst of the church. In other words, it takes place in the worship of the church. Also, Hebrews 13:15 points out that the sacrifice of praise offered to God should be the fruit of our lips: "By him therefore let us offer the sacrifice of praise to God continually, that is, the fruit of *our* lips giving thanks to his name" [KJV].

Sing With the Understanding

1st Corinthians 14:15 points out that prayer and music in worship are to be understood: "What is it then? I will pray with the spirit, and I will pray with the understanding also: I will sing with the spirit, and I will sing with the understanding also" (KJV). We can understand prayers and singing provided the words are in a language we understand. Not so with instrumental music, because there are no words to be understood.

No Inference or Example

In chapter one, it was mentioned that the Bible authorizes by command, approved apostolic example, and necessary inference. As stated previously in this chapter, the NT gives a specific command to sing in the worship of the church. However, nowhere in the New Testament do you find an approved apostolic example, or a necessary inference teaching that the church is authorized to play mechanical instruments of music in worship.

2nd Timothy 3:16-17 states: "16 All scripture *is* given by inspiration of God, and *is* profitable for doctrine, for reproof, for correction, for instruction in righteousness: 17 That the man of God may be perfect, throughly furnished unto all good works" [KJV]. Since the scriptures furnish us unto all good works, why are mechanical instruments of music in worship not mentioned in the entire NT? The only reasonable conclusion is that the use of mechanical instruments in worship is not considered a good work by God because He has not authorized such in the NT.

Source of Faith

The source of biblical faith must be the word of God: "So then faith *cometh* by hearing, and hearing by the word of God" [Romans 10:17 KJV]. If our worship to God is not according to faith, it is sinful: "for whatsoever *is* not of faith is sin" [Romans 14:23 KJV]. Although the context of

Romans 14:23 is warning Christians not to cause a weak brother to stumble, the principle that whatsoever is not of faith [approved by God's word] is sin applies to other situations as well. The point being: Mechanical instruments of music in worship are not authorized in the NT scriptures; therefore, their use is not of faith based upon God's word and is therefore sinful.

In Conclusion

According to John 4:24, Christians must worship God in spirit [from the heart] and in truth [according to His word]. God's word has authorized Christians to sing in worship, but has not authorized them to play mechanical instruments of music in worship. Those who use mechanical instruments in worship are manifesting a lack of respect for biblical authority, which is in reality a lack of respect for God.

Review

1.   Singing is a form or type of ________________.

2.   Music can be produced by either mechanical instruments or ______________ ________________.

3.   When God said that the priests were to be selected from the tribe of Levi, He didn't have to say that priests should not be selected from the other __________________.

4.   Jesus could not serve as our high priest without a change of the ____________.

5.   The silence of the New Testament relative to mechanical instruments in conjunction with the command to sing prohibits the use of mechanical instruments in __________________.

6.   The only instrument authorized to make music in New Testament worship is the ________________.

7.   There is no approved apostolic example or necessary inference in the New Testament authorizing the use of mechanical instruments of music in __________________.

8.   Faith that is acceptable to God comes from hearing God's ______________.

9.   Whatever is not of faith is ______________.

10.   Those who use mechanical instruments in worship are manifesting a lack of respect for the ______________ of the scriptures.

7

FROM WORDS ALONE DETERMINE IF IT'S WORSHIP ***TO*** LISTENING TO A HYMN IS WORSHIP

The Doctrine Pendulum

The doctrine pendulum swings from one extreme to the other with the scriptural truth lying somewhere between the two extremes. On one extreme is the opinion that words of a song alone determine if scriptural worship is involved. On the other extreme is the opinion that listening to a hymn on the radio is worship. However, the truth about worship is derived from God's word and not the opinions of men.

Old Testament Worship

Although Christians are not bound by the Old Testament [OT] systems [Mosaical and Patriarchal], Romans 15:4 indicates that we can learn from the things that are written during those time periods: "4For whatsoever things were written aforetime were written for our learning, that we through patience and comfort of the scriptures might have hope" [KJV]. What principles do the things written aforetime teach about worship?

Genesis 22:2-5 describes God's instruction and Abraham's worship to God: "2And he said, Take now thy son, thine only *son* Isaac, whom thou lovest, and get thee into the land of Moriah; and offer him there for a burnt offering upon one of the mountains which I will tell thee of. 3 And Abraham rose up early in the morning, and saddled his ass, and took two of his young men with him, and Isaac his son, and clave the wood for the burnt offering, and rose up, and went unto the place of which God had told him. 4 Then on the third day Abraham lifted up his eyes, and saw the place afar off. [5] And Abraham said unto his young men, Abide ye here with the ass; and I and the lad will go yonder and worship, and come again to you" [KJV].

There are at least five principles of worship that we learn from the account in Genesis 22:2-5, 1) God told Abraham when, where, and how to worship him. 2) Abraham had the intent to worship God; it wasn't just something that happened by chance. 3) When Abraham's worship began, it was separate and apart from his routine activities. 4) Abraham's worship complied with God's instructions. 5) When Abraham's intended worship ended, he returned to the young men and continued his routine activities.

New Testament Worship

Today, God's instruction to Christians about worship is different from his instruction to Abraham because we live under the law of Christ found in the New Testament and not under the Patriarchal System. Even so, the principles related to our worship are basically the same as Abraham's worship: 1) God has told us in the New Testament when, where, and how to worship him. In John

4:24, we are told how: "God *is* a Spirit: and they that worship him must worship *him* in spirit and in truth" [KJV]. In spirit is from the heart, and in truth is according to God's word [John 17:17]. Furthermore, we are told where and when: Corporate worship of God takes place where the whole church comes together [1st Corinthians 14:23]; the when is on the first day of the week [Acts 20:7]. This is not to say that Christians can't praise and glorify God individually, but that is not the same as corporate worship. 2) Worship is separate and apart from our routine activities; it has a beginning and an end. 3) The fact that Christians come together for the purpose of worship indicates that there is intent to worship God; it is not just something that happens by chance. 4) Worship by the church must be in compliance with God's word [John 4:24]. 5) When the worship of the church is complete, the individual Christians return to their routine activities.

Two Extremes

Both of the extremes mentioned in the first paragraph of this chapter ["words of a song alone determine if scriptural worship is involved" and "listening to a hymn on the radio is worship"] violate the principles learned from our consideration of Genesis 22.

When the principles of hermeneutics are applied to interpretation of scripture, reason and logic must be a part of the process. From a logical standpoint, it is reasonable to say that words alone determine whether a song is of a religious nature or not. However, is it logical to say that words alone determine if scriptural worship is involved? Obviously, there is more to scriptural worship than just pronouncing words that are of a religious nature.

For example, an individual may be attempting to memorize the words of a hymn or a Bible verse. Pronouncing the words over and over again would be a part of one's service to God, but would it be scriptural worship? In other words, all worship is service to God, but not all service is worship to God. Increasing our knowledge of God's word and putting it into practice as we go about our routine activities glorifies God, but is it worship? In order for worship to be involved, there has to be intent to worship. If there is intent to worship, then it must be in harmony with the New Testament scriptures.

Worship that is in harmony with God's word has a beginning and end, because it is not intended to be a part of our routine activities.

If an individual is having a difficult time resisting temptation, the first thing that should come to their mind is to pray to God for help. When their prayerful attitude leads to a silent prayer as they go about their routine activities, is it worship or part of their service to God? It has already been said that there must be intent to worship and that worship must have a beginning and an end that separates it from routine activities.

Likewise, the opinion that listening to a hymn on the radio must be construed as worship based upon Colossians 3:16 is neither logical nor reasonable. Colossians 3:16 states: 'Let the word of Christ dwell in you richly in all wisdom; teaching and admonishing one another in psalms and hymns and spiritual songs, singing with grace in your hearts to the Lord'" [KJV].

From a logical standpoint, any attempt to apply Colossians 3:16 to listening to a hymn on the radio would of necessity have to show who was being taught and admonished by the listener since this verse mentions "teaching and admonishing one another." From a biblical standpoint, the suggestion that listening to a hymn on the radio must be construed as scriptural worship ignores the principles of worship that was learned from Genesis 22:2-5.

If routinely listening to a religious song on the radio is to be considered worship, then using the same logic would require that routinely drinking grape juice [without intent to worship] would be considered partaking of the Lord's Supper. Without the intent to worship, the above mentioned acts are just part of routine activities included in our service to God.

In Conclusion

This writer would never encourage anyone to violate his conscience. If anyone believes it is a sin to listen to a hymn accompanied by a mechanical instrument on the radio, then he should not do so. However, it might be the case that some additional teaching is needed in order to make sure the conscience is properly trained. Always keep in mind that a Christian's worship must be from the heart and comply with God's instructions in the New Testament. God has told us when, where, and how to worship Him. There must be intent on our part to worship God; it isn't just something that happens by chance. Corporate worship has a beginning and an ending, because it is separate and apart from our routine activities.

Review

1. Since Christians are not bound by the Old Testament, there aren't any principles we can learn from its writings. True/False

2. It was Abraham's intent to worship God when he proceeded to offer Isaac as a sacrifice. True/False

3. Abraham's worship to God included all of his routine activities. True/False

4. Corporate worship by the church must be in compliance with New Testament scriptures. True/False

5.	There is more involved with scriptural worship than just pronouncing words that are of a religious nature. True/False

6.	Worship doesn't have a beginning and an end, but includes all of a Christian's routine activities. True/False

7.	Routinely listening to a religious song on the radio isn't worship any more than routinely drinking grape juice [without the intent to worship] is partaking of the Lord's Supper. True/False

8.	If anyone believes that it is sinful to listen to a religious song accompanied by a mechanical instrument, they should not violate their conscious. True/False

9.	Christian worship must be from the heart. True/False

10.	Colossians 3:16 doesn't support the belief that listening to a religious song on the radio is worship. True/False

8

FROM WIDOWS CAN MARRY ANYONE *TO* THEY MUST MARRY CHRISTIANS

The Doctrine Pendulum

The doctrine pendulum swings from one extreme to the other with the scriptural truth lying somewhere between the two extremes. On one extreme is the opinion that a Christian whose spouse has died can marry anyone with God's approval. On the other extreme is the opinion that a

Christian who is a widow can only marry another Christian. Nevertheless, the truth about marriage is determined by God's word and not the opinions of men.

God's Marriage Law

In Matthew 19:4-6, Jesus explained God's marriage law to the Pharisees: "And he answered and said unto them, Have ye not read, that he which made *them* at the beginning made them male and female, 5And said, For this cause shall a man leave father and mother, and shall cleave to his wife: and they twain shall be one flesh? 6 Wherefore they are no more twain, but one flesh. What therefore God hath joined together, let not man put asunder" [KJV]. In 1st Corinthians 7:39, Paul further explains God's marriage law by discussing the marriage of widows: "The wife is bound by the law as long as her husband liveth; but if her husband be dead, she is at liberty to be married to whom she will; only in the Lord" [KJV].

Only in the Lord

The phrase "only in the Lord" qualifies the statement "she is at liberty to be married to whom she will." In other words, she can only marry the person she chooses provided the qualification specified by the phrase "only in the Lord" is met. Some students of the Bible believe that the phrase "only in the Lord" indicates she can only marry another Christian. Their understanding is that "in the Lord" means the same as "in Christ".

There is no doubt that to be "in Christ" is to be a Christian. Galatians 3:26-27 states: "[26] For ye are all the children of God by faith in Christ Jesus. [27] For as many of you as have been baptized into Christ have put on Christ" [KJV]. However, does "in Christ" mean the same thing as "in the Lord"? As stated previously, both the definition of words and their context [immediate & remote] must be considered to determine the proper interpretation and be able to see the complete picture.

In the immediate context of 1 Corinthians 7:39, Paul uses the phrase "in the Lord" in verse 22, which states: "For he that is called in the Lord, *being* a servant, is the Lord's freeman: likewise also he that is called, *being* free, is Christ's servant" (KJV). Verse 22 is speaking of one that is called to be a Christian by the gospel [2nd Thessalonians 2:14]. Thus, one that is "called in the Lord" is called according to the will of God [the gospel]. It should be clear to the discerning mind that alien sinners are called in the Lord [according to the gospel] and not those who are already in Christ [Christians]. At the same time, it could be said that a Christian was called [past tense] in the Lord [according to the gospel]

A remote context for "in the Lord" [1 Corinthians 7:39] is found in Ephesians 6:1, which states: "Children, obey your parents in the Lord: for this is right." If the terminology "in the Lord" in this passage meant "Christian", the implication would be that children do not have to obey unless their parents are Christians. Therefore, it must be construed to mean that children are to obey their parents according to the will of God. Neither the immediate nor the remote context given for 1 Corinthians 7:39 indicate that the phrase "in the Lord" means the same as "in Christ" or "Christian".

The Gospel Advocate Commentaries [GAC] indicate that the restriction "only in the Lord" [1 Corinthians 7:39] "prohibits the widow marrying one not a Christian." However, the GAC then states: "I know no reason why a widow should be more restricted as to whom she marry than a virgin. This restriction however, together with the general principles laid down regulating the association of Christians with unbelievers, indicates that it was not contemplated that Christians should marry those not in the Lord."

In what appears to be an inclusion of 1 Corinthians 6:14 in the "principles regulating the association of Christians with unbelievers," the GAC indicates that "To be unequally yoked would be to be so connected with an unbeliever that she would be controlled by the unbeliever." The GAC then states: "While I would not say that this passage is an absolute prohibition of the marriage of a believer to an unbeliever, it certainly discourages it."

In view of 1 Corinthians 6:14, which states: "Be ye not unequally yoked together with unbelievers"(KJV), it would be advisable for a Christian widow to marry another Christian because of the potential for being unequally yoked with an unbeliever, but to say that it is mandatory is another matter altogether.

In addition to those previously mentioned, there are numerous passages in Paul's epistles where "in the Lord" means according to God's will instead of meaning Christian. If the terminology "only in the Lord" meant Christian instead of according to God's will, then 1 Corinthians 7:39 would prohibit a Christian widow from marrying a non-Christian. However, since the immediate and remote context indicates that "only in the Lord" means according to God's will, the widow can only be required to marry someone who was a proper candidate for marriage from a scriptural standpoint. Even so, it would be advisable that she marry a Christian.

Marriage Candidates

Regardless of whether the person considering marriage is someone who has never been married before, a divorcee, or a widow, he or she needs to make sure both parties listed on the marriage certificate [assuming there is one] are scriptural candidates for marriage. There are three categories of people who can marry with God's approval.

The first category involves a person who has never been married before. In 1 Corinthians 7:8-9, Paul stated: "[8] I say therefore to the unmarried and widows, It is good for them if they abide even as I. [9] But if they cannot contain, let them marry: for it is better to marry than to burn" (KJV). Then in verses 27 & 28 he said: "[27]Art thou bound unto a wife? Seek not to be loosed. Art thou loosed from a wife? Seek not a wife. [28] But and if thou marry, thou hast not sinned; and if a virgin marry, she hath not sinned. Nevertheless such shall have trouble in the flesh: but I spare you" (KJV). Paul wanted the unmarried to be spared the current problems that would arise from the responsibilities of marriage. Nevertheless, he advised that those who had never been married were free to marry without committing sin.

The second category involves a person whose spouse has died. In Romans 7:2, Paul said: "For the woman which hath an husband is bound by the law to *her* husband so long as he liveth; but if the husband be dead, she is loosed from the law of *her* husband" (KJV). Like those who have never been married, the widow is free to marry without committing sin [1st Corinthians 7:8].

The third category involves a person who divorced his spouse because of fornication on the part of his spouse. Jesus gives the exception to God's marriage law in Matthew 19:9, which states: "And I say unto you, Whosoever shall put away his wife, except *it be* for fornication, and shall marry another, committeth adultery: and whoso marrieth her which is put away doth commit adultery" (KJV). Like those who have never been married and those who are widows, the innocent party who has divorced his spouse because of fornication is free to remarry without committing sin. However, the party that is guilty of fornication commits adultery when remarried [Matthew 19:9] and continues to commit adultery until the adulterous relationship is ended. The guilty party who was divorced because of fornication is not free to remarry.

In all three of the previous categories, the individuals are free to marry "only in the Lord". In other words, they are free to marry with God's approval provided the circumstances of their marriage are in harmony with God's word. To the contrary, those who fail to marry in the Lord continue to commit sin as long as they remain in the marriage.

Living in Fornication

Jesus' exception to God's marriage law brings to mind the claim of some Bible students that the fornication mentioned in Matthew 19:9 is a one-time act that occurs when the marriage vows are made. According to their understanding, the couple can repent of the one-time act and continue to live in the marriage relationship without sinning, because fornication is not a sin that one lives in. Evidently they are not considering Colossians 3:5-7 which states: "5Mortify therefore your members which are upon the earth; fornication, uncleanness, inordinate affection, evil concupiscence, and covetousness, which is idolatry: 6 For which things' sake the wrath of God cometh on the children of disobedience: 7 In the which ye also walked some time, when ye lived in them" (KJV). Verse five lists fornication as one of the sins they had previously lived in before becoming a Christian. As long as a couple continues to live in an adulterous relationship, they continue to live in sin. Baptism does not make an adulterous relationship legitimate.

In Conclusion

Generally speaking, "in the Lord" as used in New Testament scriptures indicates that whatever is under consideration is according to the will of the Lord. When the text is about how one becomes a

Christian [e.g., "called in the Lord," 1st Corinthians 7:22 (KJV)], the meaning is that one is called to be a Christian according to the will of God [i.e., according to the gospel].

Review

1. From the beginning, how long is a married person bound to their spouse? _______________

    ____

2. What phrase qualifies the statement "she is at liberty to be married to whom she will" in 1st Corinthians 7:39? _______________________

    ____

3. To be in Christ is to be a Christian. True/False

4. One that is "called in the Lord" is called according to the will of God [the gospel]. True/False

5. "Children, obey your parents in the Lord" does not mean that children only have to obey if the parents are Christians. True/False

6.   In many of Paul's epistles, "in the Lord" means the same as in harmony with God's _____________.

7.   A widow can only be required to marry someone who was a proper candidate for marriage from a scriptural standpoint. True/False

8.   There are three categories of people who can marry with God's approval. True/False

9.   As long as a couple continues to live in an adulterous relationship, they continue to live in _________.

10.   Baptism does not make an adulterous relationship legitimate. True/False

9

FROM HETEROSEXUAL FORNICATION *TO* HOMOSEXUAL FORNICATION

The Doctrine Pendulum

The doctrine pendulum swings from one extreme to the other with the scriptural truth lying somewhere between the two extremes. On one extreme is the opinion that fornication committed by people in heterosexual relationships should be tolerated in a free society as long as it is between consenting adults. On the other extreme is the opinion that fornication committed by people in homosexual relationships should be tolerated in a free society as long as it is between consenting adults.

Abstain From Fornication

Living in a free society doesn't mean that you are free to do anything you want to, because every civil government places some restrictions on its citizens. Although God has ordained civil governments to protect the good and punish the evil [1 Peter 2:13-14], He doesn't approve of everything that is done or allowed by those governments. Even though the laws of civil government may not prohibit fornication, God's law prohibits every type of fornication. This is evidenced by 1 Thessalonians 4:3, which indicates: "3For this is the will of God, *even* your sanctification, that ye should abstain from fornication" (KJV). Notice that it is not a particular type that should be abstained from, but fornication in general.

Reason for Abstinence

One reason fornication should be abstained

from is indicated in 1 Corinthians 6:9-11, which states: "9 Know ye not that the unrighteous shall not inherit the kingdom of God? Be not deceived: neither fornicators, nor idolaters, nor adulterers, nor effeminate, nor abusers of themselves with mankind, 10Nor thieves, nor covetous, nor drunkards, nor revilers, nor extortioners, shall inherit the kingdom of God. 11And such were some of you: but ye are washed, but ye are sanctified, but ye are justified in the name of the Lord Jesus, and by the Spirit of our God" (KJV). According to verse 9, unrighteous people including fornicators will not inherit the kingdom of God.

Types of Fornication

In the broadest sense of the word, fornication includes all types of illicit sexual relations. Adultery, abusers of themselves with mankind, the effeminate, and idolatry are listed separately as types of fornication in 1 Corinthians 6:9. Adultery is a type of fornication where a married person has sexual relations with someone who is not his spouse. Both abusers of themselves with mankind and the effeminate are types of fornication that involves the practice of homosexuality.

Even idolatry can be defined as spiritual adultery. 1st Corinthians 6:11 points out that some of the Corinthians were fornicators. However, they changed their way of living when they became Christians. Like the Corinthians, anyone who desires to be pleasing to God and enter His kingdom must abstain from all types of fornication.

Jude 1:7 indicates that Sodom and Gomorrah were destroyed by fire because of homosexuality: "7 Even as Sodom and Gomorrah, and the cities about them in like manner, giving themselves over to fornication, and going after strange flesh, are set forth for an example, suffering the vengeance of eternal fire." At this point, it needs to be pointed out that the terminology "going after strange flesh" has reference to the practice of homosexuality.

The terminology "going after strange flesh" is described as "leaving the natural use" in Romans 1:24-27 (KJV), which states: "24Wherefore God also gave them up to uncleanness through the lusts of their own hearts, to dishonor their own bodies between themselves: 25Who changed the truth of God into a lie, and worshipped and served the creature more than the Creator, who is blessed for ever. Amen. 26For this cause God gave them up unto vile affections: for even their women did change the natural use into that which is against nature: ²⁷And likewise also the men, leaving the natural use of the woman, burned in their lust one toward another; men with men working that which is unseemly, and receiving in themselves that recompence of their error which was meet."

The term "strange" is also used in Leviticus 10:1, which states: "And Nadab and Abihu, the sons of Aaron, took either of them his censer, and put fire therein, and put incense thereon, and offered strange fire before the LORD, which he commanded them not." The fire was referred to as "strange" because it was fire that God had not commanded [authorized] them to use.

Likewise the flesh in Jude 1:7 was referred to as "strange", because God had not commanded or authorized males going after [having sex with] other males, or females having sex with other females for that matter. According to God's marriage law, it is natural for a man to marry and have sex with a woman, but "strange" to have sex outside marriage between a man and a woman.

The only sexual relationship that is approved by God is within the confines of a scriptural marriage between a man and a woman as indicated in Matthew 19:4-6, "[4]And he answered and said unto them, Have ye not read, that he which made *them* at the beginning made them male and female, [5]And said, For this cause shall a man leave father and mother, and shall cleave to his wife: and they twain shall be one flesh? [6]Wherefore they are no more twain, but one flesh. What therefore God hath joined together, let not man put asunder" (KJV).

Living Together

Since the only intimate relationship acceptable to God is one between a male and female who are scripturally married, engaging in premarital sex is sinful. This is true regardless of whether a couple is living together or not. Living together without the benefit of marriage is quite common in today's society.

Sometimes the claim is made that the intimate relationship is a trial to see if they are compatible before making a permanent commitment. Although the need for determining compatibility is extremely important, it doesn't justify living together prior to marriage, at least not in the mind of God.

In some cases, the couple living together

simply is not interested in a permanent relationship. Either they are not aware of God's marriage law stated in Matthew 19:4-6, or they simply don't care.

Any Sin Separates

Isaiah 59:2 states: "But your iniquities have separated between you and your God, and your sins have hid *his* face from you, that he will not hear" (KJV). From God's point of view, any sin [including fornication] will separate the individual from Him. However, from man's point of view some sins have greater consequences than others. For example, the sin of fornication may lead to an unwanted pregnancy, which can be devastating to an unwed mother. On the other hand, the sin of lying may not seem to harm anyone. Regardless of its physical consequence, any unforgiven sin will spiritually separate individuals from God.

God's Solution

God not only condemns fornication, but He specifies a type of sexual intimacy that is acceptable to him by inspiring the apostle Paul to write in 1 Corinthians 7:8-9, "[8]I say therefore to the unmarried and widows, It is good for them if they abide even as I ⁹But if they cannot contain, let them marry: for it is better to marry than to burn" (KJV). Under the difficult circumstances they were enduring, it was better not to take on the responsibilities of marriage by remaining celibate, provided they were able to control their sexual desires. However, if they were not able to control their sexual desires, it was better for them to marry than to burn with lust. In other words, sexual desires fulfilled within the confines of a marriage between a man and a woman avoids the sin of fornication.

In Conclusion

In a free society you will commonly find two extremes: One claiming that heterosexual fornication should be tolerated while the other claims that homosexual fornication [practice of homosexuality] should be tolerated. The truth according to God's word is that every type of fornication is sinful and must be avoided if we want to be pleasing to God. Relative to sexual intimacy, celibacy and marriage between a man and a woman are the only two choices that are acceptable to God.

Review

1. According to 1st Peter 2:13-14, God has ordained civil governments for what purpose? ______________________

   ____

2. What types of fornication are prohibited by God's law? ______________________

3. According to 1st Corinthians 6:9, what will not be inherited by fornicators and those who commit other types of sin? ______________________

   ____

4. What was the reason Sodom and Gomorrah were destroyed by fire? ______________________

   ____

5. Why was the fire mentioned in Leviticus 10:1 referred to as strange fire? ______________________

   ____

6. In Jude 1:7, what does "going after strange flesh" have reference to? ______________________

____

7. What is the only sexual relationship that is approved by God? ______________________

____

8. According to Isaiah 59:2, what separates man from God? ______________________

9. In some difficult circumstances it may be better not to take on the responsibilities of marriage, but what should a couple do if they can't control their sexual desires? __________

____

10. Relative to sexual intimacy, what are the only two choices that are acceptable to God? ______

____

10

FROM INFANT BAPTISM *TO* ADULT BAPTISM BY SPRINKLING OR POURING

The Doctrine Pendulum

The doctrine pendulum swings from one extreme to the other with the scriptural truth lying somewhere between the two extremes. On one extreme is the opinion that baptism of infants by sprinkling or pouring is necessary in order for them to be in a saved condition. On the other extreme is the opinion that baptism of adults by sprinkling or pouring will result in their sins being forgiven.

Scriptural Authority

These extreme opinions about baptism exist in part due to a lack of respect for the authority of the scriptures. In order to accurately determine God's will on any spiritual matter, the Bible student must realize that Bible doctrine takes president over the creeds of men. Furthermore, it is helpful to know that the Bible provides its own best commentary.

Modes of Baptism

When the Lord's church was first established, it wasn't necessary to discuss the modes of baptism because sprinkling and pouring did not exist at the time. Less than 200 years later there were at least three methods of baptism. Bible doctrine had not changed, so the variants in baptism would have to be attributed to the opinions of men. For anyone who is interested in obeying the will of God, the Bible clearly describes the purpose and form of baptism.

Purpose of Baptism

The purpose of baptism is indicated in the first gospel sermon recorded in Acts chapter two.

"Then Peter said unto them, Repent, and be baptized every one of you in the name of Jesus Christ for the remission of sins, and ye shall receive the gift of the Holy Ghost" (Acts 2:38 KJV). Although the purpose of baptism can be determined utilizing the English text, it is sometimes enlightening to consider the Greek text. The English word "for" in Acts 2:38 is translated from the Greek word "εις," which can be defined as "to, into, unto, toward, or for." The English word "for" indicates the purpose of baptism, which is remission or forgiveness of sins. The English words "to, into, unto, or toward" indicates that baptism moves the penitent believer toward or into the remission of sins. Therefore, the penitent believer has not obtained forgiveness of sins prior to baptism.

Form of Baptism

The form of baptism is indicated in Romans 6:3-4 (KJV). "3 Know ye not, that so many of us as were baptized into Jesus Christ were baptized into his death? 4 Therefore we are buried with him by baptism into death: that like as Christ was raised up from the dead by the glory of the Father, even so we also should walk in newness of life." Not only do these verses indicate that they were baptized into Christ, where all spiritual blessings are found (Ephesians 1:3), but they were buried with Christ by baptism. Since baptism is described as a burial, which involves a complete covering, sprinkling and pouring of water do not meet the biblical requirements for baptism.

Baptismal Candidates

Who then should be baptized or who is a proper candidate for baptism according to the Bible? Acts 8:36-37 (KJV) states: "36 And as they went on their way, they came unto a certain water: and the eunuch said, See, here is water; what doth hinder me to be baptized? 37 And Philip said, If thou believest with all thine heart, thou mayest. And he answered and said, I believe that Jesus Christ is the Son of God". Verse 37 in conjunction with Acts 2:38 indicate that only penitent believers are proper candidates for baptism.

Infant Baptism

Infants would not be candidates for baptism since they are incapable of believing or repenting.

The idea that infants need to be baptized stems from the belief that infants are guilty of original sin inherited at birth, which is sometimes called total depravity. This belief is refuted by Ezekiel 18:20 (KJV), which states: "The soul that sinneth, it shall die. The son shall not bear the iniquity of the father, neither shall the father bear the iniquity of the son." Iniquity is synonymous with sin. Therefore, the infant child is not guilty of the sins of their father or ancestors. Children are guilty in God's eyes when they commit sin themselves after reaching the age of accountability.

Jesus' Earthly Ministry

During His earthly ministry Jesus espoused the same doctrine taught by His apostles following the establishment of the church. In the words of Jesus: "He that believeth and is baptized shall be saved; but he that believeth not shall be damned" (Mark 16:16 KJV). Jesus also said: "I said therefore unto you, that ye shall die in your sins: for if ye believe not that I am he, ye shall die in your sins" (John 8:24 KJV) and "I tell you, Nay: but, except ye repent, ye shall all likewise perish" (Luke 13:3 KJV).

Apostles' Doctrine

1 John 1:7 (KJV) indicates that the blood of Christ cleanses us of all sin: "But if we walk in the light, as he is in the light, we have fellowship one with another, and the blood of Jesus Christ his Son cleanseth us from all sin."

However, the cleansing takes place when we are baptized as evidenced by Ananias' question to Paul: "And now why tarriest thou? arise, and be baptized, and wash away thy sins, calling on the name of the Lord" (Acts 22:16 KJV).

1 Peter 3:21 (KJV) confirms the purpose of baptism: "The like figure whereunto even baptism doth also now save us (not the putting away of the filth of the flesh, but the answer of a good conscience toward God,) by the resurrection of Jesus Christ."

No doubt, the answer or response of a good conscience is obedience as evidenced by Hebrews 5:8-9 (KJV), which states: "8 Though he were a Son, yet learned he obedience by the things which he suffered; 9 And being made perfect, he became the author of eternal salvation unto all them that obey him."

In Conclusion

Baptism is for the remission of sins and is reserved for penitent believers, which excludes infants. Furthermore, baptism is a burial, not a sprinkling or pouring. When we obey Jesus by repenting and being baptized, the blood of Christ cleanses us of sin. Needless to say, the Christian must remain faithful until death in order to receive eternal life (Revelation 2:10).

Review

1. When the Lord's church was first established, baptism by _______________ and _______________ did not exist.

2. The Bible clearly describes the _______________ and _______________ of baptism.

3. Acts 2:38 indicates that baptism is _______________ the remission of sins.

4. The Greek word "εις," which is translated "for" in Acts 2:38 (KJV), indicates that the one being baptized is moving _______ , _________ , __________ , or _____________ the remission of sins.

5. The penitent believer has not obtained forgiveness of sins prior to _________________.

6. In Romans 6:4, baptism is described as a _________________.

7. Acts 8:37 in conjunction with Acts 2:38 indicate that infants are not candidates for baptism because they are incapable of _________________ or _____________________.

8. According to Ezekiel 18:20 (KJV), the infant child is not guilty of the ___________ of their ancestors.

9. According to 1 John 1:7, the _____________ of Christ cleanses us of all sin.

10. According to Acts 22:16, cleansing (washing away) of sin occurs when we're ______________.

11

***FROM* OLD TESTAMENT IS BINDING TODAY *TO* NEW TESTAMENT EPISTLES ARE JUST LOVE LETTERS**

The Doctrine Pendulum

The doctrine pendulum swings from one extreme to the other with the scriptural truth lying somewhere between the two extremes. On one extreme is the opinion that the Old Testament is binding on Christians today as a law they must live by. On the other extreme is the opinion that the New Testament epistles are just love letters and do not include commandments that are binding upon Christians.

Biblical Time Periods

Biblical history can be divided into three time periods based upon how God dealt with mankind. In the first time period God dealt with mankind through the heads of households such as Adam, Abraham, Isaac, etc. This period is referred to as the Patriarchal Age and lasted from creation to the giving of the Law of Moses. The second period is the Mosaical Age, which lasted from the giving of the Law of Moses on Mount Sinai to the death of Jesus on the cross. The third time period is the Christian Age, which will last from the death of Christ until the end of time.

Mosaical Age

The Law of Moses was a covenant made by God with Moses and the Israelite nation. When Moses was on Mount Sinai receiving what is referred to as the Law of Moses, which included the

Ten Commandments, the Bible states: "And the LORD said unto Moses, Write thou these words: for after the tenor of these words I have made a covenant with thee and with Israel" (Exodus 34:27 KJV). Since the covenant was between God and the Israelite nation only, which included Moses, it should be obvious that Gentiles were not included. Furthermore, people living in the Patriarchal and the Christian Ages were not included in this covenant. Therefore, Christians are not bound by the Law of Moses as a law they must live by.

The Ten Commandments

Some who embrace the idea that the Ten Commandments are binding upon Christians claim that the Ten Commandments are distinct or separate from the law or covenant made with Israel. Their claim is false based upon Exodus 34:28 (KJV), which states: "And he was there with the LORD forty days and forty nights; he did neither eat bread, nor drink water. And he wrote upon the tables the words of the covenant, the ten commandments." The Ten Commandments were definitely a part of the covenant God made with Israel and no one else.

Christian Age

The Law of Moses including the Ten Commandments was abolished when Jesus died on the cross, which is the same time the New Testament or covenant took effect or was in force. Both Colossians 2:14 (KJV) and Ephesians 2:15 (KJV) respectively speak of the end of the Law of Moses: "Blotting out the handwriting of ordinances that was against us, which was contrary to us, and took it out of the way, nailing it to his cross," and "Having abolished in his flesh the enmity, even the law of commandments contained in ordinances; for to make in himself of twain one new man, so making peace."

Hebrews 9:15-17 (KJV) speaks of the beginning of the Christian Age, which was the time when the New Testament or covenant took effect: "15 And for this cause he is the mediator of the new testament, that by means of death, for the redemption of the transgressions that were under the first testament, they which are called might receive the promise of eternal inheritance. 16 For where a testament is, there must also of necessity be the death of the testator. 17 For a testament is of force after men are dead: otherwise it is of no strength at all while the testator liveth." Thus, the New Testament took effect when Jesus, its testator, died on the cross.

New Testament Law

Jesus is the mediator of the new covenant or testament, which is referred to as the law of the Spirit of life in Christ Jesus in Romans 8:2 (KJV): "For the law of the Spirit of life in Christ Jesus hath made me free from the law of sin and death." The law of sin and death is a reference to the Law of Moses.

The new covenant is also referred to as the perfect law of liberty in James 1:25 (KJV): "But whoso looketh into the perfect law of liberty, and continueth therein, he being not a forgetful hearer, but a doer of the work, this man shall be blessed in his deed."

The apostle Paul sought to serve all men by preaching the gospel of Christ, but his primary focus was preaching the gospel to the Gentiles. In 1 Corinthians 9:21 (KJV) he speaks of the Gentiles, who were without the Law of Moses: "To them that are without law, as without law, (being not without law to God, but under the law to Christ,) that I might gain them that are without law."

To summarize the three previous verses, Christians are not bound by the Law of Moses, but they are bound by the law of Christ. The New Testament is Christ's covenant with Christians, who are bound by its precepts.

Just Love Letters

Throughout the history of the Lord's church there have been apostates who were guilty of teaching false doctrine, such as the assertion that the New Testament epistles are just love letters and do not include commandments that are binding on Christians. In order to support their assertion, it was necessary for its promoters to establish a new hermeneutics.

In the 1993 issue of The Spiritual Sword Wayne Jackson expounds on "The Crisis of a New Hermeneutic." His discussion includes several premises contained in the so called new hermeneutic, three of which are listed below:

1. "Second, the 'new hermeneutic' contends that no doctrine can be made a test of fellowship that has been arrived at through the process of logical reasoning. This includes such matters as the use of

mechanical instruments of music in Christian worship.[7] Rational thinking has given way to subjectivism."

2. "Third, it is argued that our concept of respecting the 'silence of the Scriptures' has been erroneous, and that our insistence that 'necessary inference' is a valid means of determining New Testament authority has been productive of much harm.[8]"

3. "Fourth, the apostles of the 'new hermeneutic' assert that the New Testament is not a 'constitutional document'; rather it is merely a series of 'love letters' which are not to be approached in a legal fashion.[9]"

The three premises listed above fly in the face of sound biblical hermeneutics and cast doubt on the New Testament as an objective standard of authority during the Christian dispensation.

In Acts 5:29 (ASV): "Peter and the apostles answered and said, We must obey God rather than men." If we must obey God, that would most certainly include keeping his commandments. Jesus said in John 14:15 (KJV): "If you love me, keep my commandments." So what about New Testament epistles, do they include commandments of Jesus that must be kept? Paul claimed as much in 1st Corinthians 14:37 (KJV): "If any man think himself to be a prophet, or spiritual, let him acknowledge that the things that I write unto you are the commandments of the Lord."

In Conclusion

During the Patriarchal Age God dealt with mankind through the heads of the households. The Law of Moses was not given until the end of this dispensation of time, so people living during the Patriarchal Age were never amenable to the Law of Moses.

The Mosaical Age was in effect from the end of the Patriarchal Age to the beginning of the Christian Age. The Law of Moses, which included the Ten Commandments, was given to Moses and Israel. So the Gentiles were not amenable to the Law of Moses during the Mosaical Age.

The Christian Age began at the death of Christ and will last until the end of time. The Ten Commandments along with the rest of the Law of Moses was abolished when Jesus died on the cross. Christians are amenable to the New Testament, which includes many of the principles taught in the

Ten Commandments, but they are not bound to keep any of the Old Testament or covenant.

The New Testament epistles are more than just love letters. They include commandments of the Lord that must be kept. Christians are bound by the New Testament's perfect law of liberty and not by the Law of Moses, which was only given to Israel.

Review

1. God has not changed but He has dealt with mankind differently during different time periods.   True/False

2. The Law of Moses was in effect from the giving of the law on Mount Sinai until the death of Jesus.   True/False

3. God's covenant that included the Ten Commandments was given to Moses and Israel only.   True/False

4. People living during the Patriarchal Age and the Christian Age were not included in the covenant given to Moses and Israel. True/False

5. The Law of Moses was blotted out or abolished when it was nailed to the cross at the time of Jesus' death.   True/False

6. The New Testament is God's covenant with Christians who are bound by its precepts. True/False

7. Some men claim that the New Testament epistles are just love letters and do not include commandments that are binding on Christians.   True/False

8. Peter and the other apostles said that we must obey God rather than men.   True/False

9. The apostle Paul stated that his writings or epistles were the commandments of the Lord. True/False

10. Christians are under law to Christ, which is the perfect law of liberty.   True/False

12

FROM CHURCH WAS AN AFTERTHOUGHT _TO_ KINGDOM WILL BE ESTABLISHED WHEN JESUS RETURNS

The Doctrine Pendulum

The doctrine pendulum swings from one extreme to the other with the scriptural truth lying somewhere between the two extremes. On one extreme is the opinion that Jesus was not able to establish an earthly kingdom, so as an afterthought,

He established the church. On the other extreme is the opinion that His earthly kingdom will be established when Jesus returns.

Church's Eternal Purpose

The idea that Jesus came to establish His kingdom, but was rejected by the Jews so He established the church as an afterthought, is not supported by scripture. Speaking to members of the church at Ephesus, Paul stated: "4 According as he hath chosen us in him before the foundation of the world, that we should be holy and without blame before him in love: 5 Having predestinated us unto the adoption of children by Jesus Christ to himself, according to the good pleasure of his will," (Ephesians 1:4-5 KJV). The Ephesian Christians were chosen by God before the foundation of the world to be adopted by Jesus.

Paul continues in Ephesians 3:10-11 (KJV) to explain God's eternal purpose for establishing the church: "10 To the intent that now unto the principalities and powers in heavenly places might be known by the church the manifold wisdom of God, 11 According to the eternal purpose which he purposed in Christ Jesus our Lord." The church was not an afterthought, but was established according to God's eternal purpose in order to make known the manifold wisdom of God.

The predestination mentioned in Ephesians 1:5 isn't the false Calvinistic doctrine that God chooses some to be saved and others to be lost without giving the individuals a choice in the matter. Romans 8:30 in conjunction with 2nd Thessalonians 2:14 explains that God predestined or pre-determined before the foundation of the world that individuals would be called by the gospel of Christ and chosen to salvation through sanctification of the Spirit and belief of the truth. Furthermore, Christ "became the author of eternal salvation unto all them that obey him," (Hebrews 5:9 KJV).

Church Synonymous with Kingdom

In Matthew 4:17 (KJV) Jesus indicated that the kingdom was about to be established: "From that time Jesus began to preach, and to say, Repent: for the kingdom of heaven is at hand." He further stated that the kingdom would be established during the lifetime of some of His audience: "And he said unto them, Verily I say unto you, That there be some of them that stand here, which shall not taste of death, till they have seen the kingdom of God come with power," (Mark 9:1 KJV).

The terms church and kingdom are used interchangeably in scripture. In Matthew 16:18-19 (KJV) Jesus said: "18 And I say also unto thee, That thou art Peter, and upon this rock I will build my church; and the gates of hell shall not prevail against it. 19 And I will give unto thee the keys of the kingdom of heaven: and whatsoever thou shalt bind on earth shall be bound in heaven: and whatsoever thou shalt loose on earth shall be loosed in heaven." In other words, the church that Jesus built is the kingdom (of heaven) on earth. The apostles were given the keys of the kingdom to open the door of the church by preaching the gospel.

The church was established in Jerusalem on the first Pentecost following Jesus' ascension into heaven as described in Acts chapter two. Later Paul indicated that he and members of the church at Colosse were already part of the kingdom: "Who hath delivered us from the power of darkness, and hath translated us into the kingdom of his dear Son," (Colossians 1:13 KJV). Prior to His ascension,

Jesus used parables to teach about the mysteries of the coming kingdom.

Parables

A parable is a physical story that conveys a spiritual principle. It is often described as "an earthly story with a heavenly meaning." Jesus used the parable as a form of teaching so that those who were receptive to the truth would understand or would ask for an explanation, while those who were not receptive to the truth would not understand nor be interested in an explanation.

For example, Luke 8:8-10 (KJV) states: "8And other fell on good ground, and sprang up, and bare fruit an hundredfold. And when he had said these things, he cried, He that hath ears to hear, let him hear. 9And his disciples asked him, saying, What might this parable be? 10And he said, Unto you it is given to know the mysteries of the kingdom of God: but to others in parables; that seeing they might not see, and hearing they might not understand." Anyone who is receptive to the truth will properly discern for themselves or ask for assistance, because they have a desire to know and do the will of God.

When analyzing a parable, some Bible

students attempt to equate everything in the illustration with something in the spiritual principle(s) being taught. In the parable of the ten virgins, the kingdom of heaven has something in common with the illustration of the bridegroom and virgins. However, not everything about the wedding feast is exactly the same as the kingdom of heaven. The ten virgins needed to be prepared for the coming of the bridegroom, because they did not know when he would arrive. Likewise, all members of the church need to be prepared for the coming of Christ, because they do not know when He will arrive.

In one of His many parables describing His kingdom Jesus compares the kingdom to leaven, which illustrated the massive influence the church would have on the whole world during the first century and beyond: "Another parable spake he unto them; The kingdom of heaven is like unto leaven, which a woman took, and hid in three measures of meal, till the whole was leavened," [Matthew 13:33 KJV]. In this case, the parable is an extended simile.

Simile

A simile describes one thing by stating that it is "like" or "as" something else. It doesn't mean they are exactly the same, but there is a similarity. For example, in Isaiah 1:18 (KJV), the LORD describes sin by saying: "though your sins be as scarlet, they shall be as white as snow; though they be red like crimson, they shall be as wool." The difference in the colors red and white draw a contrast between an individual's condition before and after forgiveness takes place. A simile is another way of helping us paint a mental picture in order to expand our understanding.

Numerous other verses describe what the church/kingdom would be like. The Bible student is encouraged to use a concordance in search of other verses that describe the Lord's church.

Second Coming of Jesus

Jesus will be coming back, but it won't be for the purpose of establishing His kingdom. Instead, He will deliver the kingdom to the Father as indicated in 1st Corinthians 15:24 (KJV): "Then cometh the end, when he shall have delivered up the kingdom to God, even the Father; when he shall have put down all rule and all authority and power."

How do we know that Jesus won't come back to the earth, establish His kingdom, and then deliver it to the Father? For one reason, we've already learned from scripture that Jesus' church/kingdom was established just after his ascension into heaven. Secondly, there is no indication in the scriptures that Jesus will ever set foot on the earth again: "16 For the Lord himself shall descend from heaven with a shout, with the voice of the archangel, and with the trump of God: and the dead in Christ shall rise first: 17 Then we which are alive and remain shall be caught up together with them in the clouds, to meet the Lord in the air: and so shall we ever be with the Lord, (1st Thessalonians 4:16-17 KJV).

In Conclusion

The New Testament scriptures use the terms church and kingdom interchangeably indicating that Jesus' church and kingdom are synonymous with one another. His church/kingdom was established on the first Pentecost following Jesus' ascension into heaven. Therefore, Jesus won't be coming back to establish His kingdom. Furthermore, Jesus won't ever set foot on this earth again. Faithful members of His church/kingdom will be caught up to meet Him in the clouds and so shall they ever be with the Lord in heaven.

Review

1. The idea that Jesus came to establish His kingdom, but established the church as an afterthought when the Jews rejected Him, is not supported by scripture.   True/False

2. When were the Ephesian Christians chosen by God to be adopted by Christ?   _______________

     ____

3. God's manifold wisdom was to be made known by the church according to His _______________ purpose.

4. God pre-determined before the foundation of the world that individuals would be called by the gospel of Christ.   True/False

5.   To whom did Jesus become the author of salvation? ______________________

____

6.   Jesus said that some in His audience would not taste of death until they have seen the ______________ ______ ________ come with power.

7.   The terms church and kingdom are used interchangeably in scripture.   True/False

8.   Paul indicated that the Colossian Christians were already part of the ______________.

9.   When Jesus returns, to whom will He deliver the kingdom? ______________________

10.   When Jesus returns, He will not set foot on the earth, but the faithful will be caught up to meet the Lord in the air.   True/False

13

FROM THE BEGINNING *TO* THE END

The Doctrine Pendulum

From the beginning of this book to the end, the doctrine pendulum has swung from one extreme to the other with the scriptural truth lying somewhere between the two extremes. There seems to be no end to the list of extremes. Every example of false extremes points out the need for proper interpretation of scripture in order to establish the truth.

Helps and Hindrances

Preconceived ideas and personal opinions can be a hindrance to the Bible student. On the other hand, understanding the difference between literal and symbolic language, using parallel versions and passages, and understanding figures of speech can be useful in ascertaining the message God intended to be gleaned from His word.

Literal Versus Symbolic

How can the Bible student determine if a scripture is literal or symbolic? A scripture is symbolic when a literal translation demands something that is wrong, forbids something that is right, or causes a contradiction between scriptures. Furthermore, it should be obvious that a scripture is figurative if the inspired writer says that it is.

Parallel Versions

Reading several parallel versions of the Bible can be a help, provided the versions are word translations and not thought translations. Word translations utilize English words that adequately represent the Greek text, while thought translations sometimes substitute the translator's thoughts [opinions] in place of a proper translation of the Greek text.

For example, the opinion that "unworthily" in 1st Corinthians 11:29 pertains to the worthiness of the person partaking of the Lord's Supper is a preconceived idea that will hinder you from properly interpreting this scripture. 1st Corinthians 11:27-29 (KJV) states: "27Wherefore whosoever shall eat this bread, and drink *this* cup of the Lord, unworthily, shall be guilty of the body and blood of the Lord. 28But let a man examine himself, and so let him eat of *that* bread, and drink of *that* cup. 29For he that eateth and drinketh unworthily, eateth and drinketh damnation to himself, not discerning the Lord's body."

The King James Version uses the term "unworthily" while the American Standard Version uses the terminology "in an unworthy manner". So from a comparison of the two versions you can see that verses 27 and 29 are speaking of the manner in which the worshiper partakes and not the worthiness of the partaker. The Christian partakes in an unworthy manner when he does not discern the body of Christ, which means he does not consider the suffering Jesus endured on the cross. The context of verses 27 and 29 specifically deals with abusing the Lord's Supper by making a common meal of it and not discerning the Lord's body.

In the English text the grammatical construction of verses 27 and 29 indicates that "unworthily" is an adverb that modifies the verbs "eateth and drinketh". The word "unworthily" is not an adjective that could describe the worthiness of the person partaking, because adjectives never end with a "ly." Likewise, in the Greek text the word "αναξιως" that is translated "unworthily" in the KJV is an adverb that describes the verbs eateth and drinketh. Therefore, the adverb "αναξιως" is properly translated "unworthily" or "in an unworthy manner."

Parallel Passages

Parallel passages in the same version of the Bible can be a help to the Bible student in properly interpreting the scriptures. For example, some Bible students have a misunderstanding of Matthew 26:26 (KJV), which states: "And as they were eating, Jesus took bread, and blessed *it*, and brake *it*, and gave *it* to the disciples, and said, Take, eat; this is my body." Since the KJV translation uses the terminology "and blessed *it*," many Christians ask God to bless the bread as they often do when eating a meal. The fact that "*it*" is italicized indicates that it was not in the Greek text. So when Jesus "blessed," what was He actually doing?

Luke 22:17-20 (KJV) provides a more easily understood translation when it says: "[17]And he took the cup, and gave thanks, and said, Take this, and divide *it* among yourselves: [18]For I say unto you, I will not drink of the fruit of the vine, until the kingdom of God shall come. [19]And he took bread, and gave thanks, and brake *it*, and gave unto them, saying, This is my body which is given for you: this do in remembrance of me. [20]Likewise also the cup after supper, saying, This cup *is* the new testament in my blood, which is shed for you." Verse 19 says that Jesus took bread and gave thanks. When you parallel this verse with verse 26 of Matthew chapter 26, it is evident that Jesus was giving thanks when He "blessed." The previous verses show that the term "blessed" can be used interchangeably with "gave thanks". According to "Strong's Talking Greek Hebrew Dictionary," the Greek word translated "blessed" is derived "from a compound of G2095 (eu) and G3056 (logos); to *speak well of,* i.e. (religiously) to *bless* (*thank* or *invoke a benediction upon, prosper*) :- bless, praise." In other words, it means to praise or thank God for something.

Therefore, when 1 Corinthians 10:16 (KJV) makes reference to the fruit of the vine: "The cup of blessing which we bless, is it not the communion of the blood of Christ? The bread which we break, is it not the communion of the body of Christ," it is implying that we bless or thank God for the fruit of the vine [cup]. The previous explanation is not suggesting that it is wrong to ask God to bless the bread and fruit of the vine, but to simply point out that Jesus was giving thanks for these emblems.

Figures of Speech

A lack of understanding relative to figures of speech used in the Bible can result in a misinterpretation of scripture. To the contrary, understanding figures of speech used in the Bible will be helpful in properly interpreting the scriptures. The following material names, defines, and gives examples of four figures of speech that have not been discussed previously.

Metaphors

A metaphor is the calling of one thing by another name that is figurative and possibly more descriptive. In Luke 13:32 (KJV), Jesus used a metaphor to describe Herod: "And he said unto them, Go ye, and tell that fox, Behold, I cast out devils, and I do cures to day and to morrow, and the third *day* I shall be perfected." The word "fox" is a metaphor for Herod indicating that he had at least one characteristic that is possessed by a fox. Herod was probably sly like a fox.

Allegories

You might say that an allegory is a metaphor that has been expanded into story form. In Matthew 9:16-17 (KJV), Jesus uses an allegory to infer the impropriety of His disciple's fasting [a sign of grief] while He was still with them. Jesus said: "[16]No man putteth a piece of new cloth unto an old garment, for that which is put in to fill it up taketh from the garment, and the rent is made worse. [17]Neither do men put new wine into old bottles: else the bottles break, and the wine runneth out, and the bottles perish: but they put new wine into new bottles, and both are preserved." In other words, just as it was inappropriate to put new cloth in an old garment, it would be inappropriate for Jesus' disciples to fast while He was still with them. The allegory is different from the metaphor in that the reader must infer the principle intended by the writer because it isn't specifically mentioned in the allegory.

Hyperboles

A hyperbole exaggerates in order to make a point more effectively. In other words, it's like saying: I'm going to the extreme just to make a point." An example is found in 1st Kings 4:29 (KJV), which states: "And God gave Solomon wisdom and understanding exceeding much, and largeness of heart, even as the sand that *is* on the sea shore." The exaggeration is the terminology "even as the sand that is on the sea shore," which is used to make the point that God blessed Solomon exceedingly.

Synecdoches

A synecdoche is the use of a part to represent the whole, or vice versa. An example is found in Acts 20:7 (KJV), which states: "And upon the first *day* of the week, when the disciples came together to break bread, Paul preached unto them, ready to depart on the morrow; and continued his speech until midnight." In this verse the terminology "break bread", which is a part of the Lord's Supper, is used to represent the Lord's Supper as a whole. The reader must not assume that these Christians only partook of the bread and excluded the fruit of the vine, because a part represents the whole.

In Conclusion

The previous material was written to illustrate interpretations based upon sound hermeneutical principles. The recommended method of interpretation is the inductive method, which is by far the best method in existence. This method is basically a gathering of all the facts before drawing a conclusion about what the Holy Spirit meant by the apostles' inspired writings.

Although the writers of scripture were inspired by the Holy Spirit, translators and interpreters are not. Therefore, it is extremely important that Bible students use dependable word translations. Thought translations could very well include opinions of men that conflict with the truth of God's word. It is also extremely important that the Bible student utilize sound principles of biblical interpretation in order to determine if what is being taught is true [Acts 17:11]. As this book is drawn to a close, be assured that God will bless all who have a proper respect for the authority of the scriptures and use sound biblical hermeneutics when interpreting scripture.

Review

1. A scripture is symbolic when a literal translation demands something that is wrong, forbids something that is right, or causes a contradiction between _____________________.

2. Thought translations sometimes substitute the translator's thoughts [opinions] in place of a proper _________________ of the Greek text.

3. Verses 27 and 29 of 1st Corinthians are speaking of the manner in which the worshiper partakes and not the worthiness of the _____________________.

4.   The Christian partakes in an unworthy manner when he does not discern the _______________ of Christ, which means he does not consider the suffering Jesus endured on the cross.

5.   When Jesus instituted the Lord's Supper, He "took bread and blessed *it*," which means He gave _______________ for the bread.

6.   In Luke 13:32, Jesus uses the word "fox" as a _______________ in reference to Herod.

7.   An allegory is a metaphor that has been _______________ into story form.

8.   A hyperbole exaggerates in order to make a _______________ more effectively.

9.   A synecdoche is the use of a _______________ to represent the whole, or vice versa.

10.   It is extremely important that Bible students use dependable _______________ translations and not thought translations.

Works Cited

"Aims and Principles." *American Atheists*. Web. 1 Jan. 2015.
<http://atheists.org/about-us/aims-and-purposes>.

Beyer, Catherine. "Deism." *About Religion*. Web. 24 Feb. 2015.
<http://altreligion.about.com/od/alternativereligionsaz/p/
Deism.htm>.

Calvin, John. "A Treatise of the Eternal Predestination of God." *Grace
Online Library*. Web. 28 Feb. 2015.
<http://www.graceonlinelibrary.org/reformed-theology/
predestination-election/a-treatise-of-the-eternal-
predestination-of-god-by-john-calvin/>.

Define Deism at Dictionary.com. Web. 24 Feb. 2015.
<http://dictionary.reference.com/browse/deism>.

Dungan, D. R. *HERMENEUTICS*. Delight, Arkansas: Gospel Light.
Print.

Gospel Advocate Commentaries. Gospel Advocate Bible Study
Library: Deluxe Ed. Gospel Advocate Company: Nashville,
TN, 2005. Computer Software.

Highers, Alan E. "I Corinthians 14:34, 35----Keep Silence. "The
Spiritual Sword. Jan. 1996. Vol. 27. p. 25. Print.

Jackson, Wayne. "The Crisis of a New Hermeneutic." *The Spiritual
Sword*. October 1993. Vol. 25. p. 25. Print.

"John Calvin on Predestination." *Theologians & Theology*. Web.
24 Feb. 2015. <http://www.theologian-theology.com/
theologians/john-calvin-predestination/>.

"John Calvin's Quotes." *Kerrigan Skelly's Blog*. Web. 28 Feb. 2015. <http://kerriganskelly.com/2014/09/01/john-calvin-quotes-the-calvinism-of-john-calvin-are-calvinists-really-calvinists/>.

Strong's Greek and Hebrew Dictionary. Gospel Advocate Bible Study Library: Deluxe Ed. Gospel Advocate Company: Nashville, TN, 2005. Computer Software.